CAMBRIDGE
Primary Computing

Learner's Book 1

Jon Chippindall, Ben Davies
& Isabella Lieghio

Shaftesbury Road, Cambridge CB2 8EA, United Kingdom

One Liberty Plaza, 20th Floor, New York, NY 10006, USA

477 Williamstown Road, Port Melbourne, VIC 3207, Australia

314–321, 3rd Floor, Plot 3, Splendor Forum, Jasola District Centre, New Delhi – 110025, India

103 Penang Road, #05–06/07, Visioncrest Commercial, Singapore 238467

Cambridge University Press is part of the University of Cambridge.

It furthers the University's mission by disseminating knowledge in the pursuit of education, learning and research at the highest international levels of excellence.

www.cambridge.org
Information on this title: www.cambridge.org/9781009296984

© Cambridge University Press & Assessment 2023

This publication is in copyright. Subject to statutory exception and to the provisions of relevant collective licensing agreements, no reproduction of any part may take place without the written permission of Cambridge University Press.

20 19 18 17 16 15 14 13 12 11 10

Printed in Poland by Opolgraf

A catalogue record for this publication is available from the British Library

ISBN 978-1-009-29698-4 Paperback with Digital Access (1 Year)
ISBN 978-1-009-29697-7 Digital Learner's Book (1 Year)
ISBN 978-1-009-29700-4 eBook

Additional resources for this publication at www.cambridge.org/go

Cambridge University Press has no responsibility for the persistence or accuracy of URLs for external or third-party internet websites referred to in this publication, and does not guarantee that any content on such websites is, or will remain, accurate or appropriate. Information regarding prices, travel timetables, and other factual information given in this work is correct at the time of first printing but Cambridge University Press does not guarantee the accuracy of such information thereafter.

....

NOTICE TO TEACHERS IN THE UK
It is illegal to reproduce any part of this work in material form (including photocopying and electronic storage) except under the following circumstances:
(i) where you are abiding by a licence granted to your school or institution by the Copyright Licensing Agency;
(ii) where no such licence exists, or where you wish to exceed the terms of a licence, and you have gained the written permission of Cambridge University Press;
(iii) where you are allowed to reproduce without permission under the provisions of Chapter 3 of the Copyright, Designs and Patents Act 1988, which covers, for example, the reproduction of short passages within certain types of educational anthology and reproduction for the purposes of setting examination questions.

....

Endorsement statement

Endorsement indicates that a resource has passed Cambridge International's rigorous quality-assurance process and is suitable to support the delivery of a Cambridge International curriculum framework. However, endorsed resources are not the only suitable materials available to support teaching and learning, and are not essential to be used to achieve the qualification. Resource lists found on the Cambridge International website will include this resource and other endorsed resources.

Any example answers to questions taken from past question papers, practice questions, accompanying marks and mark schemes included in this resource have been written by the authors and are for guidance only. They do not replicate examination papers. In examinations the way marks are awarded may be different. Any references to assessment and/or assessment preparation are the publisher's interpretation of the Cambridge International curriculum framework requirements. Examiners will not use endorsed resources as a source of material for any assessment set by Cambridge International.

While the publishers have made every attempt to ensure that advice on the qualification and its assessment is accurate, the official curriculum framework, specimen assessment materials and any associated assessment guidance materials produced by the awarding body are the only authoritative source of information and should always be referred to for definitive guidance. Cambridge International recommends that teachers consider using a range of teaching and learning resources based on their own professional judgement of their students' needs.

Cambridge International has not paid for the production of this resource, nor does Cambridge International receive any royalties from its sale. For more information about the endorsement process, please visit www.cambridgeinternational.org/endorsed-resources

Cambridge International copyright material in this publication is reproduced under licence and remains the intellectual property of Cambridge Assessment International Education.

Third-party websites and resources referred to in this publication have not been endorsed by Cambridge Assessment International Education.

Introduction

Welcome to Stage 1 of **Cambridge Primary Computing!**

There is technology all around us.

This book will help you to understand how it works.

It has lots of interesting topics and fun activities.

These will encourage you to be curious and ask lots of questions.

Questions such as:

- How many different types of computer are there?
- Do all robots look like humans?
- What is the internet and how do we connect to it?
- What does the internet allow us to do?
- How can computers help us answer questions?

You will use computing ideas for things that you do every day, such as brushing your teeth.

You will also program a Bee-Bot™ to make it move around your classroom floor, like the children are doing on the front of this book.

We learn best when we are active and working together.

The book is full of activities where you can work with a partner or a group.

There is also a special project at the end of each unit.

We hope you enjoy thinking and working like a computer scientist!

Jon Chippindall, Ben Davies and Isabella Lieghio

Contents

How to use this book 6

1 Computational thinking and programming

1.1 Algorithms all around us 9
1.2 Bee-Bot beginnings 19
1.3 What happens next? 33
1.4 Spot the bug 49

2 Managing data

2.1 Using data 60
2.2 Collecting data 75

3 Networks and digital communication

3.1 Get connected 91
3.2 Introducing the internet 102

4 Computer systems

4.1 Types of technology 113
4.2 Ins and outs 124
4.3 Bots everywhere! 135

Glossary 146
Acknowledgements 151

> Note for teachers: Throughout the resource there is a symbol to indicate where additional digital only content is required. This content can be accessed through the Digital Learner's Book on Cambridge GO. It can be launched either from the Media tab or directly from the page. The symbol that denotes additional digital content is: ⬇. The source files can also be downloaded from the Source files tab on Cambridge GO. In addition, this tab contains a teacher guidance document which supports the delivery of digital activities and programming tasks in this Learner's Book.

How to use this book

In this book you will find lots of different features to help your learning.

What you will learn in the topic. ———▶

We are going to:
- learn that many devices are controlled by computers
- identify what robots are and what they can do.

Important words to learn. ———▶

algorithm   instructions
error   sequence

A reminder about what you already know and an activity to start you off. ———▶

Getting started
What do you already know?
- Asking questions can help you learn new things.
- There are different ways of finding answers to our questions.
- You can put objects into groups.

Fun activities about computing. Sometimes, you will use a computer. ———▶

Activity 3
Get to know the Bee-Bot
You will need:
a Bee-Bot, an empty space with a smooth floor (like tiles or wood)

Work with a partner.
Look at the Bee-Bot.
1 What buttons can you see on the Bee-Bot?

Some activities do not need a computer. These are called unplugged activities. They help you to understand important ideas about computing. ———▶

Unplugged activity 2
How are they connected?
You will need:
a pencil and paper or a whiteboard pen and mini whiteboard

With your teacher, look round your classroom or library.
Find computers and devices (like printers) that are part of your school's network.
- Say the name of each device.
- Draw a picture of each device.
- Does the device use a wire to connect to the network? If it does, put a tick ✓ next to your picture.

Sometimes, you will see this question. It will help you to think about your work. ———▶

How am I doing?
- How many devices were connected by wires?
- How many devices had a wireless connection?
Share your answers with a partner.

How to use this book

Tasks to help you to practise what you have learnt.

Programming tasks are in Unit 1.

> **Programming task 1**
>
> **Program the Bee-Bot**
>
> You will need:
> a Bee-Bot, an empty space with a smooth floor (like tiles or wood)
>
> Look again at Sofia's algorithm.
>
> 1. Go forwards two steps.
> 2. Go backwards two steps.

Practical tasks are in Unit 2.

> **Practical task 1**
>
> **Add your data**
>
> You will need:
> a desktop computer or laptop with internet access, source file
> **2.1_favourites_table**
>
> Your teacher will give you a file.
>
> 1. Add the data about your favourite colour and favourite animal to the table.
> 2. Use the mouse or arrow keys to move to the correct place in the table.
> 3. Type your data.

Look out for this icon. You are going to do an activity at the computer using a source file or website link. This content can be found in the Digital Learner's Book on Cambridge GO. Your teacher will help you to get started.

Questions

Questions that help you to check that you understand the topic. Are you ready to move on?

1. A Bee-Bot turns in quarter turns.
   Zara wants the Bee-Bot to spin all the way around.
   Help her to program the Bee-Bot.
   How many turns will she need?

> **Stay safe!**
>
> Zara always checks which websites she is allowed to go on. She only goes online with a trusted adult.

Things to remember when you are using a computer.

> **Did you know?**
>
> Bee-Bots can remember up to 40 instructions at a time.
> How many instructions can you remember at a time?
> Why is it useful to remember lots of instructions?

Interesting facts connected to the topic.

7

How to use this book

Questions to help you think about how you learn. →

> Do you like learning in a group?
> Do you like playing games to learn?

What you have learnt in the topic. →

Look what I can do!
- ☐ I know that some devices can connect to each other to make a network.
- ☐ I know that devices connected to the same network can share information.
- ☐ I understand that some devices use wires to connect to a network.
- ☐ I understand that some devices do not need wires to connect to a network.

At the end of each unit, there is a project for you to carry out, using what you have learnt. You might make something or solve a problem. →

Project

Command the Bee-Bot!

You will need:
a small object (like a toy, LEGO brick or pencil), tape or a ruler

1. Find a space.
   Hide a small object a short distance away from you.
   Put something at your feet to mark the start point, like some tape or a ruler.
   Draw or write the path from the start point to the object.
   Use the commands that a Bee-Bot uses:
   - clear
   - forwards

Questions that cover what you have learnt in the unit. If you can answer these, you are ready to move on to the next unit. →

Check your progress

1. Zara, Marcus and Sofia have connected their computers together.
   What is the name for a group of computers that are connected? Choose the correct answer.
   A set
   B group
   C network
2. Arun wants to connect to the same network as his friends.
   Which objects can he use to connect to the network?

   a    b    c

1 ▶ Computational thinking and programming

❯ 1.1 Algorithms all around us

We are going to:
- learn what an algorithm is
- use an algorithm to do a task
- learn what an error is
- find an error in an algorithm.

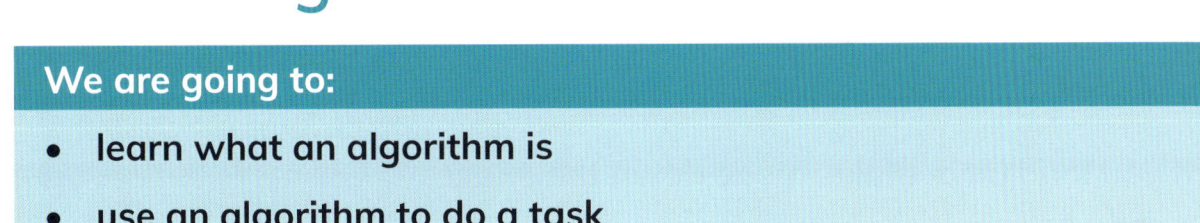

algorithm   instructions
error   sequence

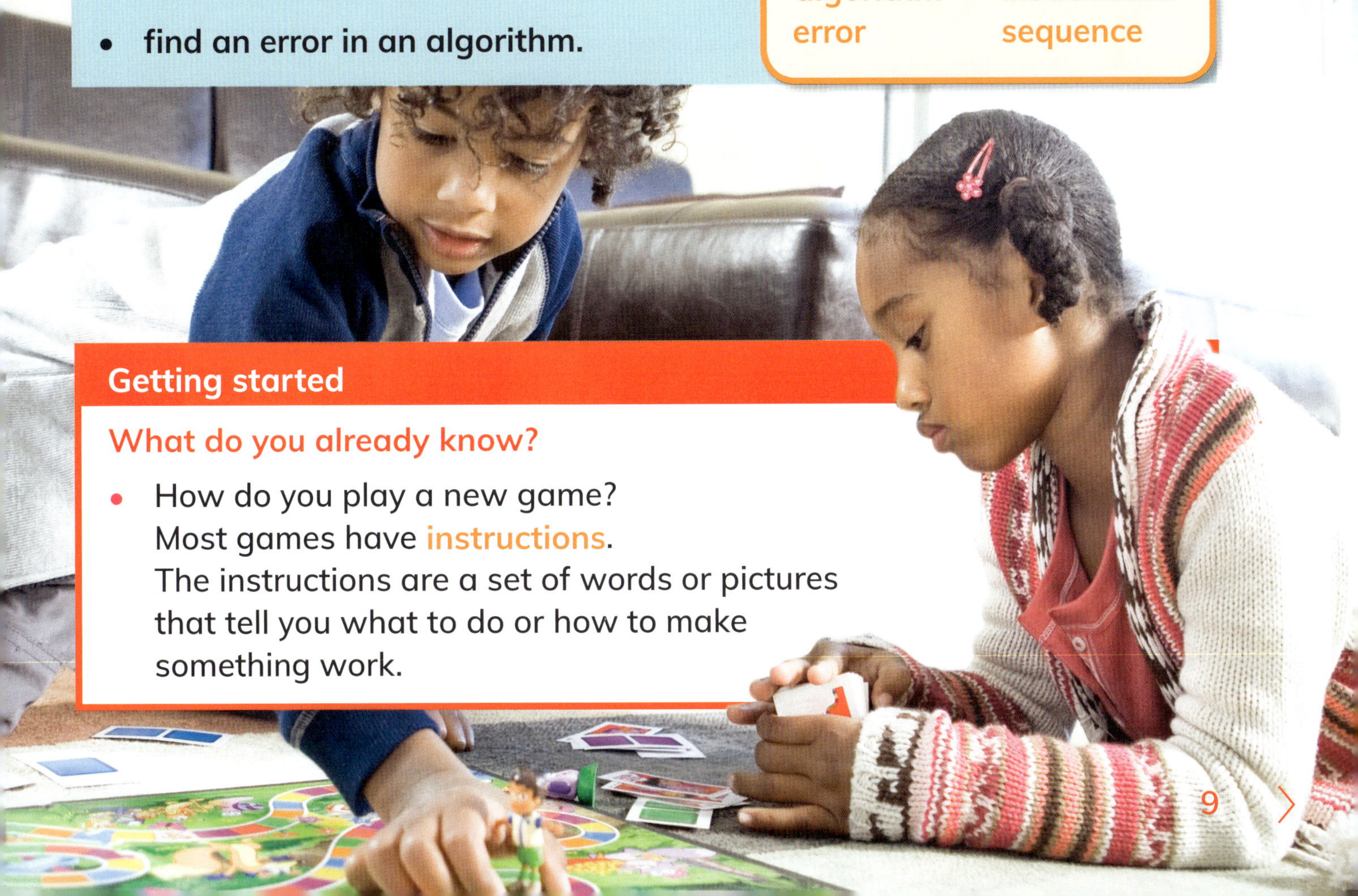

Getting started

What do you already know?
- How do you play a new game?
  Most games have **instructions**.
  The instructions are a set of words or pictures that tell you what to do or how to make something work.

1 Computational thinking and programming

Continued

Now try this!

Look at this set of instructions.

1. Spin the spinner. It will land on a number.
2. Move that number of spaces on the board.
3. If you land on a ladder, move up the ladder.

4. If you land on a snake, move down the snake.

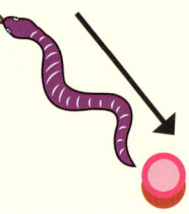

5. The winner is the first person to get to the finish square at the top of the board.

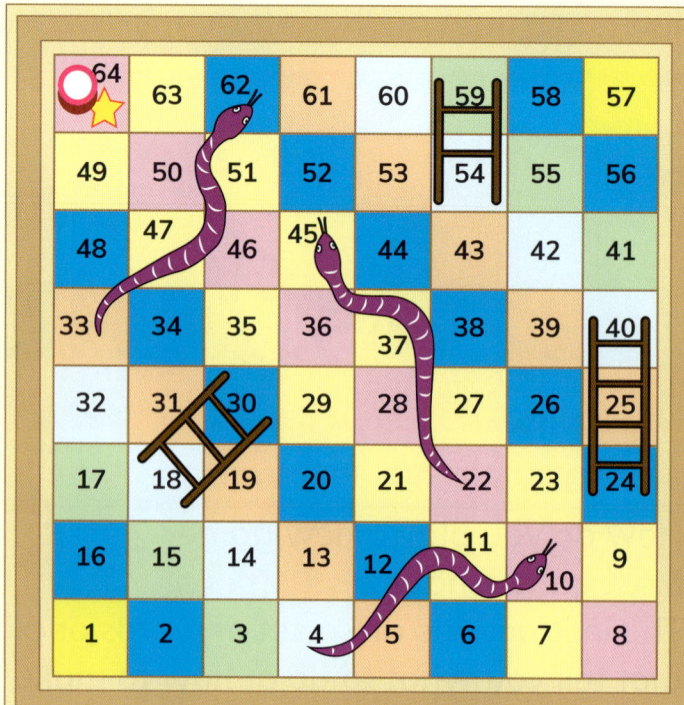

1.1 Algorithms all around us

> **Continued**
>
> Work with a partner.
>
> 1. Talk about the instructions. Do you both understand the game?
> 2. Think of three times when you followed instructions. Tell your partner about them.

"I follow instructions when I bake cakes with Dad."

What is an algorithm?

An **algorithm** is a set of instructions.

We use algorithms every day.

- We use algorithms when we get dressed.
- We use algorithms when we pack our school bags.
- We use algorithms when we eat our lunch.

1 Computational thinking and programming

The instructions in an algorithm need to be in the correct **sequence**.

This means that they need to be in the right order.

The algorithm will then work in the correct way.

You have to put your socks and shoes on in the correct order. You can't put your socks on after your shoes!

Unplugged activity 1

Follow an algorithm

> You will need:
> a sink, water, soap, paper towels

Here is an algorithm. What is it for?

1

2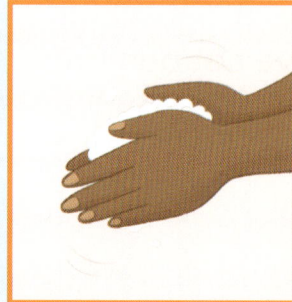

3

4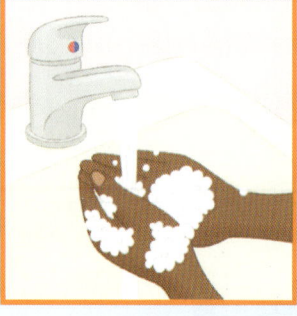

5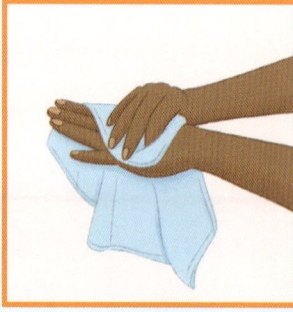

1.1 Algorithms all around us

> **Continued**
>
> Follow the algorithm.
>
> Talk with a partner.
> - Was the algorithm easy to follow?
> - Are the instructions in the correct sequence?
> - Is there anything you would add or change?

Mistakes in algorithms

When something is not correct or goes wrong, we call it a mistake.

In computing, mistakes are often called **errors**.

The algorithm may not work correctly if there is an error in it.

It is important to find the error and fix it.

Examples of errors in algorithms are:
- putting instructions in the wrong order
- missing out some of the instructions.

13

1 Computational thinking and programming

Unplugged activity 2

Find an error in an algorithm

You will need:
pencil and paper, or a whiteboard pen and mini whiteboard

A recipe tells you how to cook something.

The instructions are in the correct sequence. Remember, this means that they are in the right order.

A recipe is an algorithm.

Sofia has found an algorithm for making a pizza.

She thinks there is an error in it.

1 Make the pizza dough.

2 Make the dough flat, in the shape of a circle.

3 Add tomato sauce.

4 Add cheese.

1.1 Algorithms all around us

Continued

5   Now eat it!

6   Add toppings, such as mushrooms or peppers.

7   Cook the pizza in the oven.

Find the error in this algorithm.

Which instruction is in the wrong place?

Check with a partner to see if you found the same error.

Say the sequence in the correct order.

How am I doing?

How did you find the error in the pizza algorithm?

1 Computational thinking and programming

Now we can look at another type of algorithm.

Unplugged activity 3

Is there an error in the algorithm?

Marcus shows Arun an algorithm.

1. Get your toothbrush.

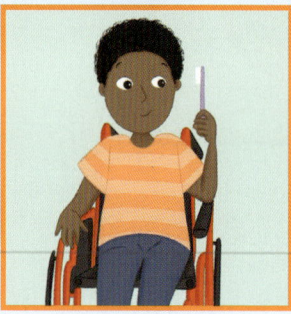

2. Brush your teeth for two minutes.

3. Rinse your mouth.

4. Rinse your toothbrush.

5. Dry your mouth.

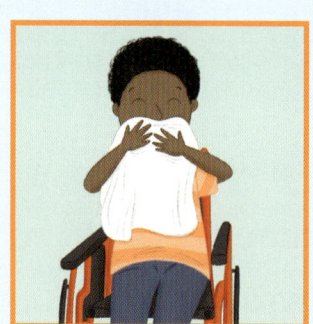

6. Put toothpaste on your toothbrush.

1.1 Algorithms all around us

Continued

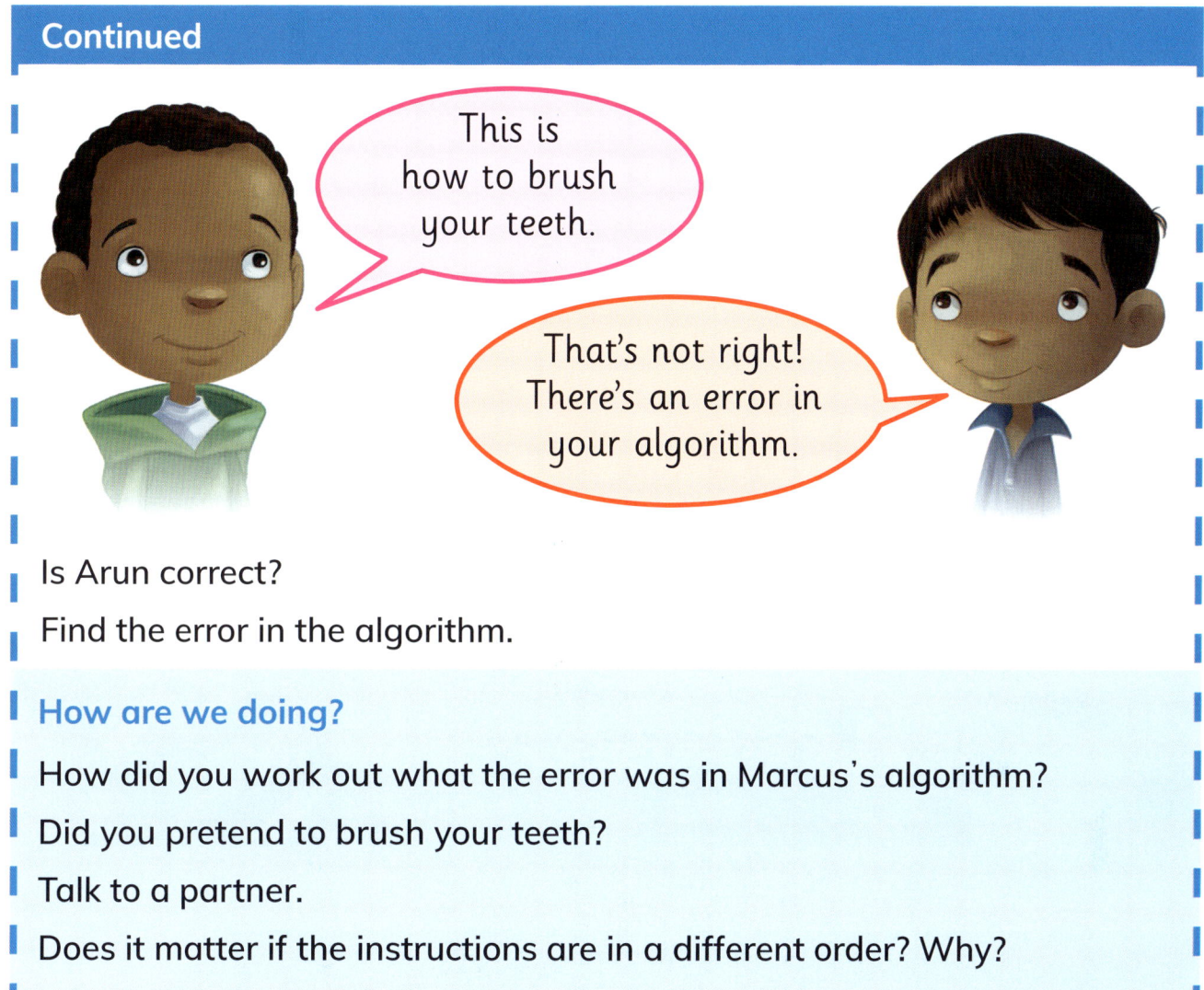

This is how to brush your teeth.

That's not right! There's an error in your algorithm.

Is Arun correct?

Find the error in the algorithm.

How are we doing?

How did you work out what the error was in Marcus's algorithm?

Did you pretend to brush your teeth?

Talk to a partner.

Does it matter if the instructions are in a different order? Why?

Questions

Think about the algorithms you use every day.

1. Name three things that algorithms help you to do.
2. How do the algorithms help you to do these things?
3. When do you use algorithms in school?

1 Computational thinking and programming

Did you know?

When we follow instructions to make a model out of LEGO bricks, we are following an algorithm!

You have learnt long words in this topic like algorithm and sequence.

How do you remember new words?

Look what I can do!

- ☐ I know that an algorithm is a set of instructions.
- ☐ I can use an algorithm to wash my hands.
- ☐ I can find errors in an algorithm.

> 1.2 Bee-Bot beginnings

We are going to:
- give a partner instructions to follow
- learn how to make a Bee-Bot move
- change an algorithm into a program.

algorithm   directions
code   instructions
command   program

Getting started

What do you already know?

- An algorithm is a set of instructions.
- An algorithm only works properly when the instructions are in the correct order.

Now try this!

Talk to a partner. How do you play with a remote-controlled car?

1. How do you make it move?
2. Which ways can the car go?

1 Computational thinking and programming

Directions

The direction is the path that the car moves along.

Draw or write down the directions that the car can move in.

When we play with a remote-controlled car, we send a message to the car to tell it to move in the correct direction.

Cars normally move forwards and backwards.

They can also turn left and right.

Give instructions

When we get lost, we ask for directions.

Directions tell us the way to go.

Directions are an algorithm.

In Topic 1.1, we learnt that an algorithm is a set of instructions.

Someone asks for directions to the hospital. You can say:

1. Go to the end of the road.
2. Turn right.
3. Go past the park.
4. The hospital is on the left.

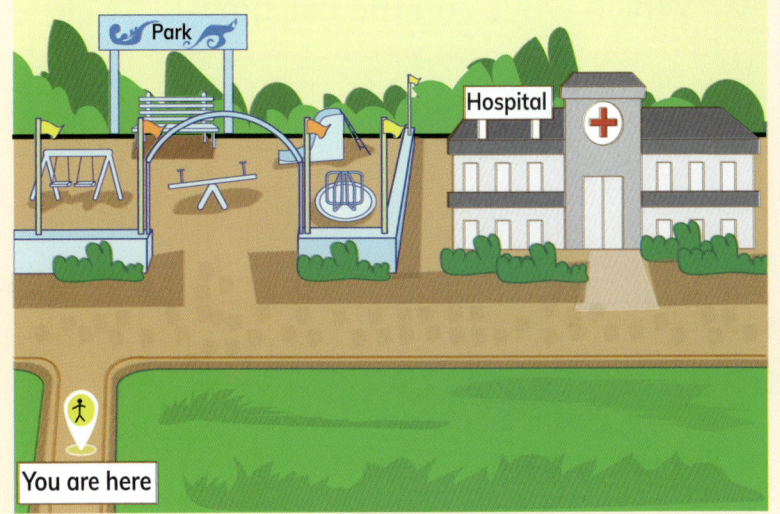

Can you follow the algorithm?

Use your finger to show the route on the map.

Quarter turns

In this topic, we will use special directions called quarter turns.

This circle is cut into four parts.

Each part is called a quarter.

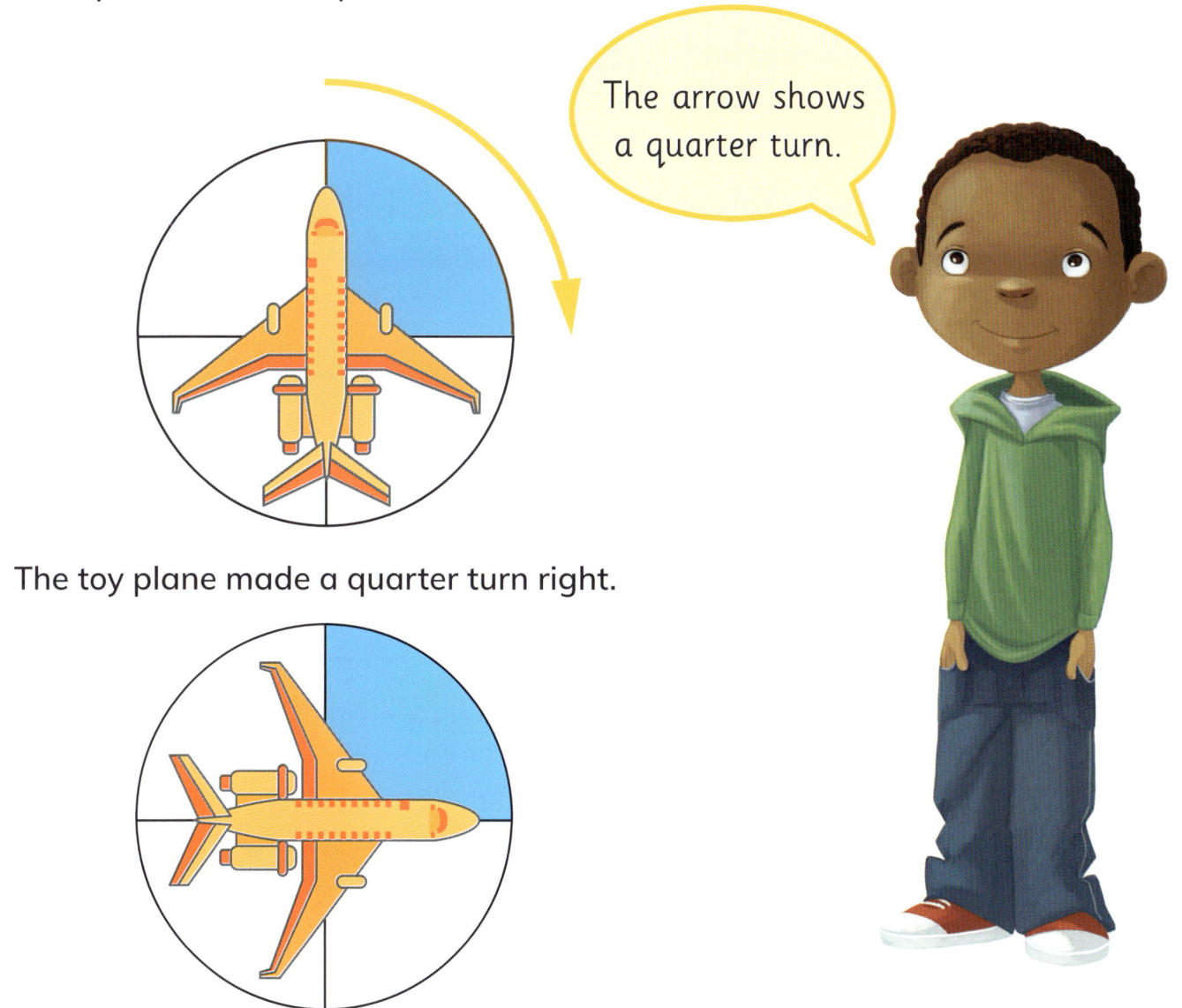

The toy plane made a quarter turn right.

The toy plane will now make a quarter turn left.

Which way will it face?

1 Computational thinking and programming

Unplugged activity 1

Help your partner to follow directions

> You will need:
> an open space, such as a playground

This algorithm asks you to follow directions.

1. Move forwards three steps.
2. Turn a quarter turn right.
3. Move forwards two steps.
4. Turn a quarter turn right.
5. Move backwards one step.

Work with a partner.

Find some space.

Take turns to give the instructions in the algorithm.

Think about where you started the algorithm.

Are you looking in the same direction now?

Can you point to the spot where you started?

1.2 Bee-Bot beginnings

Unplugged activity 2

Make your own algorithm

> You will need:
> paper, pens or pencils

Look at the grid.

Jun is at the start. He wants to get to the red balloon.

Say or write the algorithm he will need.

Use these words: forwards, backwards, left, right.

How many steps will he need to take?

Tip! One square is one step.

How are we doing?

Share your instructions for Jun with a partner.

Are your algorithms the same?

Does Jun always end at the red balloon?

Your algorithms can be different, but Jun must still get to the red balloon.

23

1 Computational thinking and programming

What is a Bee-Bot?

This is a Bee-Bot. We give it instructions to make it move.

We **program** a Bee-Bot.

This means that we put instructions into the Bee-Bot to make it do a task.

We use the buttons on the back of a Bee-Bot to program it.

Activity 3

Get to know the Bee-Bot

You will need:
a Bee-Bot, an empty space with a smooth floor (like tiles or wood)

Work with a partner.

Look at the Bee-Bot.

1. What buttons can you see on the Bee-Bot?
2. What do you think each button does?
3. Turn the Bee-Bot on. Can you make it move?

1.2 Bee-Bot beginnings

Here is a picture of the Bee-Bot.

It tells you what each button does.

Does the picture match your answers from Activity 3?

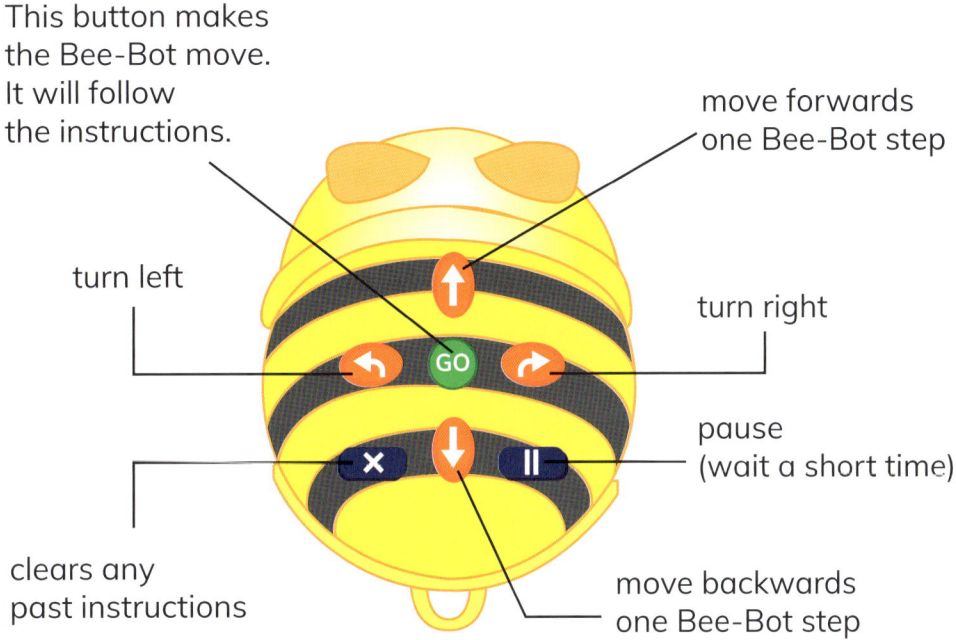

The buttons give commands to the Bee-Bot.

Commands are instructions that tell the Bee-Bot what to do.

Did you know?

When a Bee-Bot turns, it turns a quarter turn on the spot.

If you want it to move in the new direction, use the forwards command.

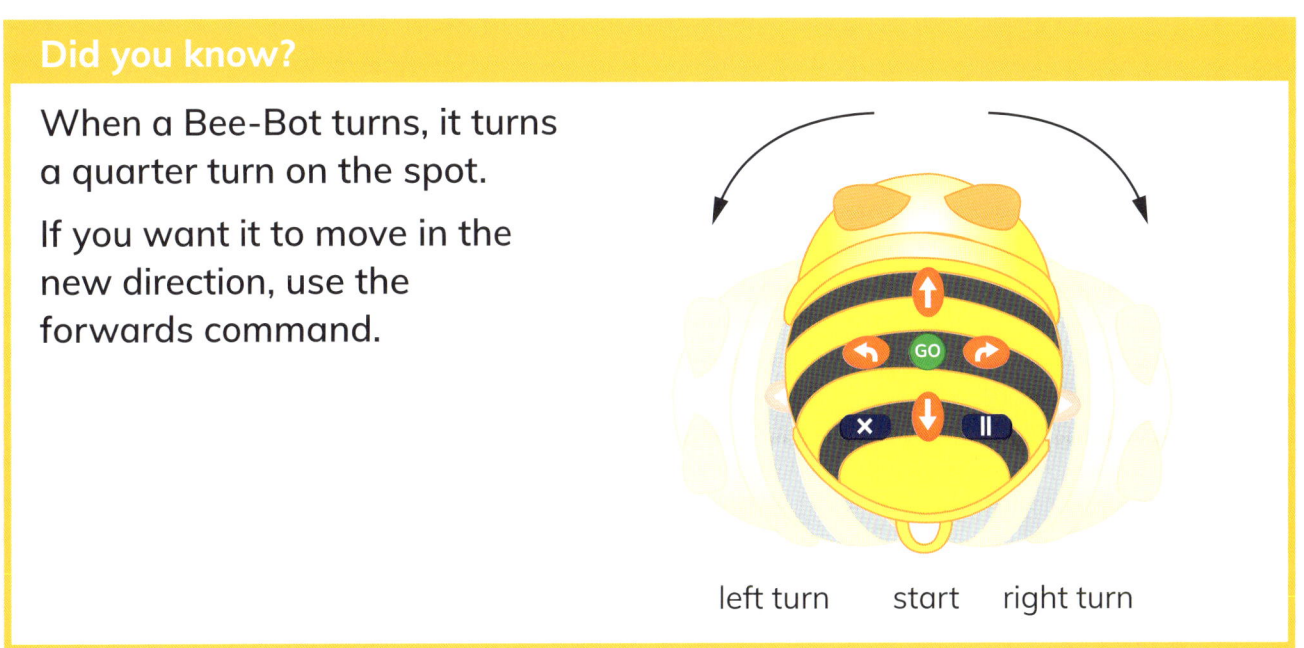

25

1 Computational thinking and programming

Unplugged activity 4

Where will the Bee-Bot go?

We need to plan where we want the Bee-Bot to go.

We can write an algorithm for that.

Sofia has written an algorithm for her Bee-Bot to follow.

1. Go forwards two steps.
2. Go backwards two steps.

Can you follow Sofia's algorithm?

Move your body to see where her Bee-Bot will go.

How will the Bee-Bot know where to go?

Now we know where we want the Bee-Bot to go.

But the Bee-Bot doesn't know yet.

We need to turn our algorithm into **code**.

When a computer gets instructions in code, it carries out the program.

A Bee-Bot does not have a brain like we do.

We have to program it using a special language.

The language is called code.

1.2 Bee-Bot beginnings

Have a look at this Bee-Bot code:

This is where the Bee-Bot would go:

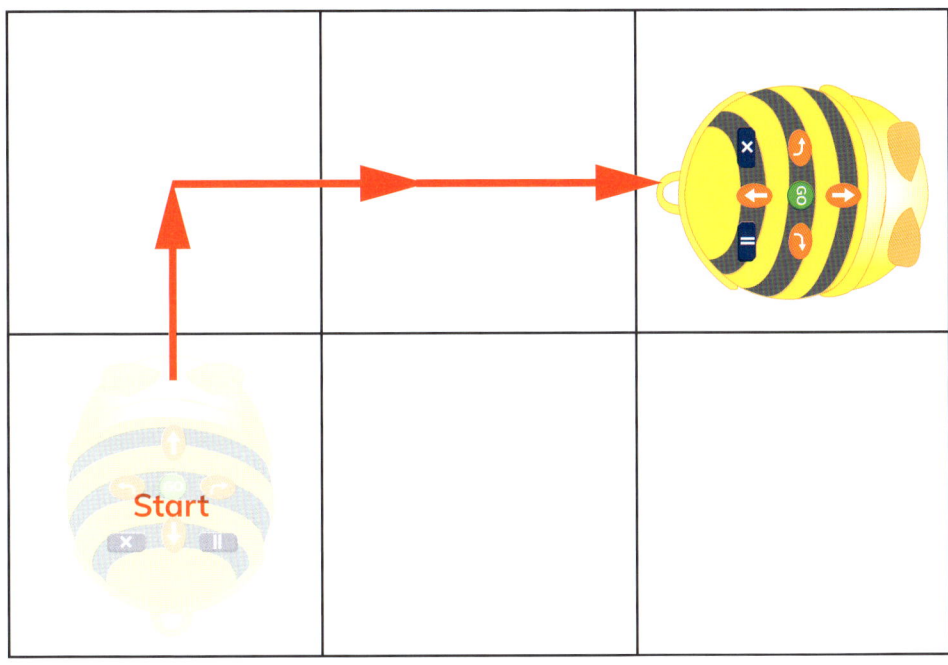

A Bee-Bot step is 15 cm.

Did you know?

Bee-Bots can remember up to 200 instructions at a time.

How many instructions can you remember at a time?

Why is it useful to remember lots of instructions?

1 Computational thinking and programming

Programming task 1

Program the Bee-Bot

> You will need:
> a Bee-Bot, an empty space with a smooth floor (like tiles or wood)

Look again at Sofia's algorithm.

1. Go forwards two steps.
2. Go backwards two steps.

Help Sofia to program her algorithm into the Bee-Bot.

1. What Bee-Bot commands does Sofia need?

   Write or say the commands.

   Remember, commands are instructions that tell the Bee-Bot what to do.

2. Program the Bee-Bot with the code.

   Don't forget:
   - Press X first to clear any past instructions.
   - Press GO when you finish programming.

3. What happened when you programmed the Bee-Bot and pressed GO?

   Did the Bee-Bot move in the direction you guessed?

4. Where did the Bee-Bot end up?

5. What did the Bee-Bot do when it finished moving?

Remember, program means to put the code into the Bee-Bot.

28

Continued

How are we doing?

Work with a partner.

Draw the Bee-Bot's command buttons on pieces of paper.

Turn them all over.

Take turns to turn over a piece of paper and look at the button.

What does the command make the Bee-Bot do? Tell your partner.

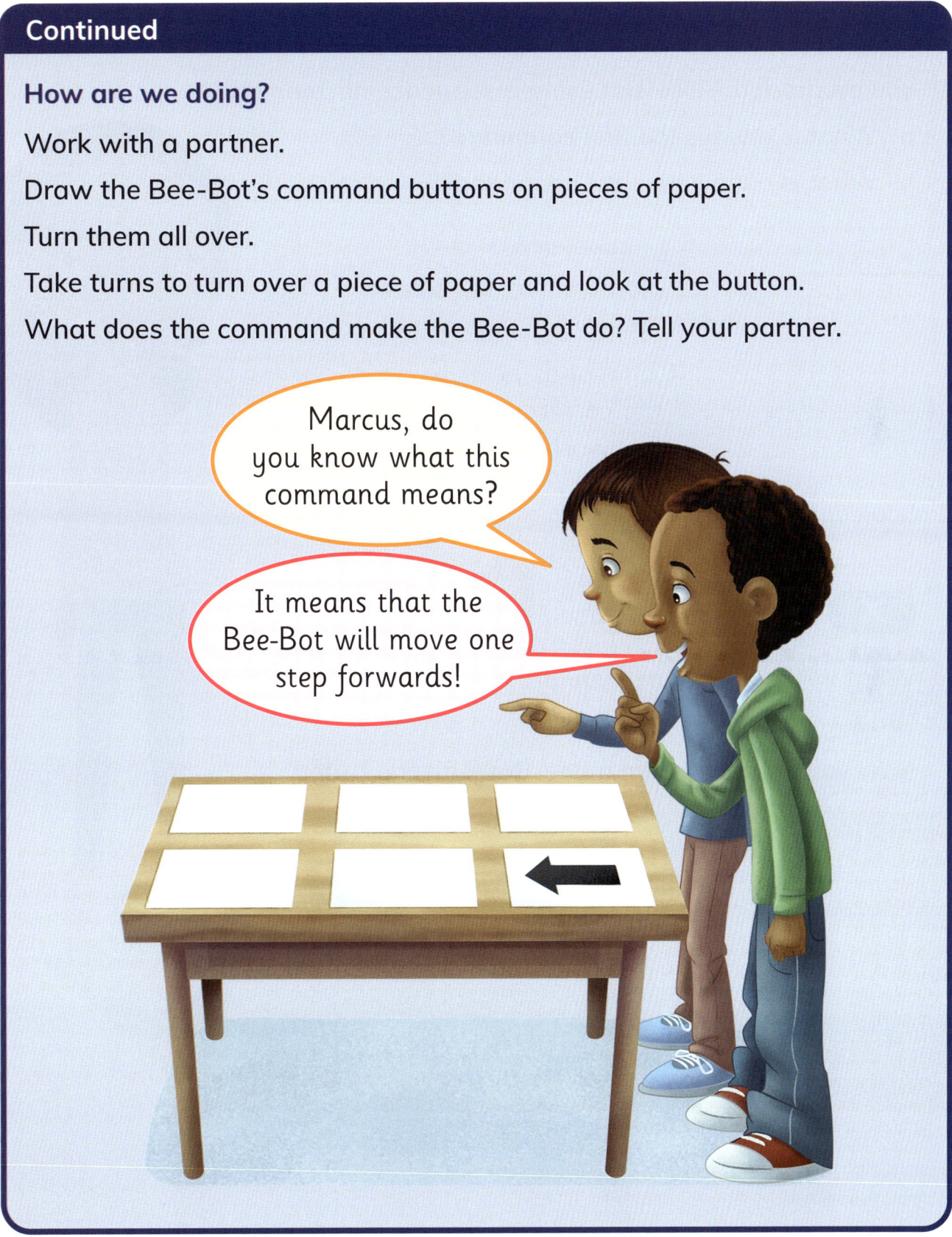

1 Computational thinking and programming

Questions

1 You program the Bee-Bot using a sequence of commands.

   a What is always the first command?

   b What is always the last command?

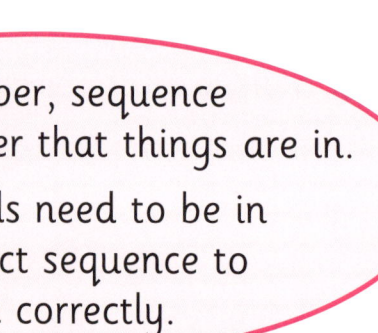

Remember, sequence means the order that things are in.

Commands need to be in the correct sequence to work correctly.

2 Look at this code.

What will happen when you program the Bee-Bot?

Draw your ideas. Share them with a partner.

Now you try it! Program a Bee-Bot with the code.

Well done! You have followed algorithms.
You have moved your body to follow directions.
You made a drawing to show what the code will do.
Which did you like doing best?

1.2 Bee-Bot beginnings

Programming task 2

Post-Bot

> You will need:
> a pencil and paper, or a whiteboard pen and mini whiteboard,
> a Bee-Bot, a Bee-Bot street grid made from source file **1.1_post_street**

The Bee-Bot is at the post office.

It is looking out to the street.

It needs to take post to the shops on the street.

Can you help it get to the right shop?

1. The Bee-Bot wants to take flour to the bakery.

   Zara has written an algorithm to help:

   > 1 Go forwards three.
   > 2 Turn right.
   > 3 Go forwards one.

   Put your finger on the post office.

   Follow the algorithm with your finger on the map.

   Does it go to the bakery?

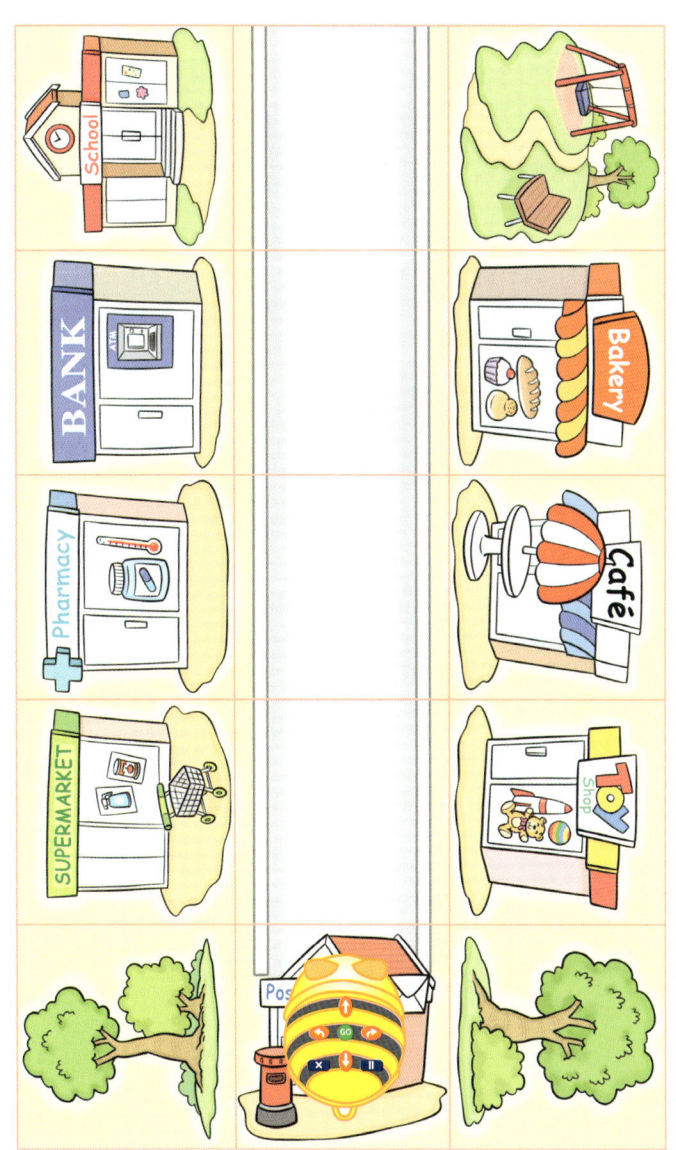

31

1 Computational thinking and programming

Continued

2. Zara then turned the algorithm into code.

Program the code into your Bee-Bot.

Does it go to the bakery?

3. The Bee-Bot is back at the post office.

Marcus has code that will take it to another shop.

Which shop will it take the Bee-Bot to?

I think the Bee-Bot will go to the café. What do you think?

Program your Bee-Bot with the code.

Were you correct?

4. The Bee-Bot would like to take a box to the toy shop.

Can you help it to get there? Write or say the code.

Program the code into your Bee-Bot.

Look what I can do!

- ☐ I can give a partner instructions to follow.
- ☐ I can make a Bee-Bot move in different directions.
- ☐ I can turn an algorithm into a program.

> 1.3 What happens next?

We are going to:

- write or draw instructions to build a brick tower
- write or draw instructions in the correct order
- make changes to algorithms
- predict what programs will do.

algorithm   predict
code   programs
command   run

Getting started

What do you already know?

- How to write or say an algorithm for a Bee-Bot.
- How to program a Bee-Bot to make it:
  - move forwards
  - move backwards
  - turn left
  - turn right.

1 Computational thinking and programming

Continued

Now try this!

Look at these instructions.

> 1 Put one hand in the air. Stretch out your fingers.
> 2 Keep your hand flat and move it to the right.
> 3 Keep your hand flat and move it to the left.
> 4 Keep moving your hand from right to left quickly.

What are the instructions asking you to do?

Follow the instructions. Were you correct?

Instructions are important!

Computers carry out instructions quickly.

The instructions need to be written clearly.

They also need to be in the correct order.

1.3 What happens next?

Unplugged activity 1

Make a brick tower

You will need:
small building bricks in different colours, a pencil and paper, or a whiteboard pen and mini whiteboard

Choose five bricks. Make sure they are a mix of different colours.

Make a tower from them.

Then follow these instructions.

1. Draw or write an algorithm for how to make your tower.

> Remember to put the instructions in the correct order.
> Start with the colour of the brick you added first.
> Here is a way: 1 Start with a blue brick.

2. Give your algorithm to a partner. Ask them to follow it.

   Do not show them your tower yet!

3. When your partner has made their tower, show them your tower.

   Do the towers look the same?

   If not, why do the towers look different?

1 Computational thinking and programming

Continued

How are we doing?

Talk to your partner.

Did they find your algorithm easy to follow?

How can you make your algorithm better next time?

Unplugged activity 2

Look at the two algorithms.

Match each algorithm with the correct paper doll.

Explain your choice to a partner.

Algorithm 1

1. Add blue trousers.
2. Add a green T-shirt.
3. Add yellow shoes.
4. Add brown hair.

Algorithm 2

1. Add blue trousers.
2. Add a red T-shirt.
3. Add yellow shoes.
4. Add black hair.

A B

1.3 What happens next?

Numbering instructions

The instructions in algorithms often start with numbers.

Why is it helpful for instructions in algorithms to have numbers?

Unplugged activity 3

Do algorithms always have words?

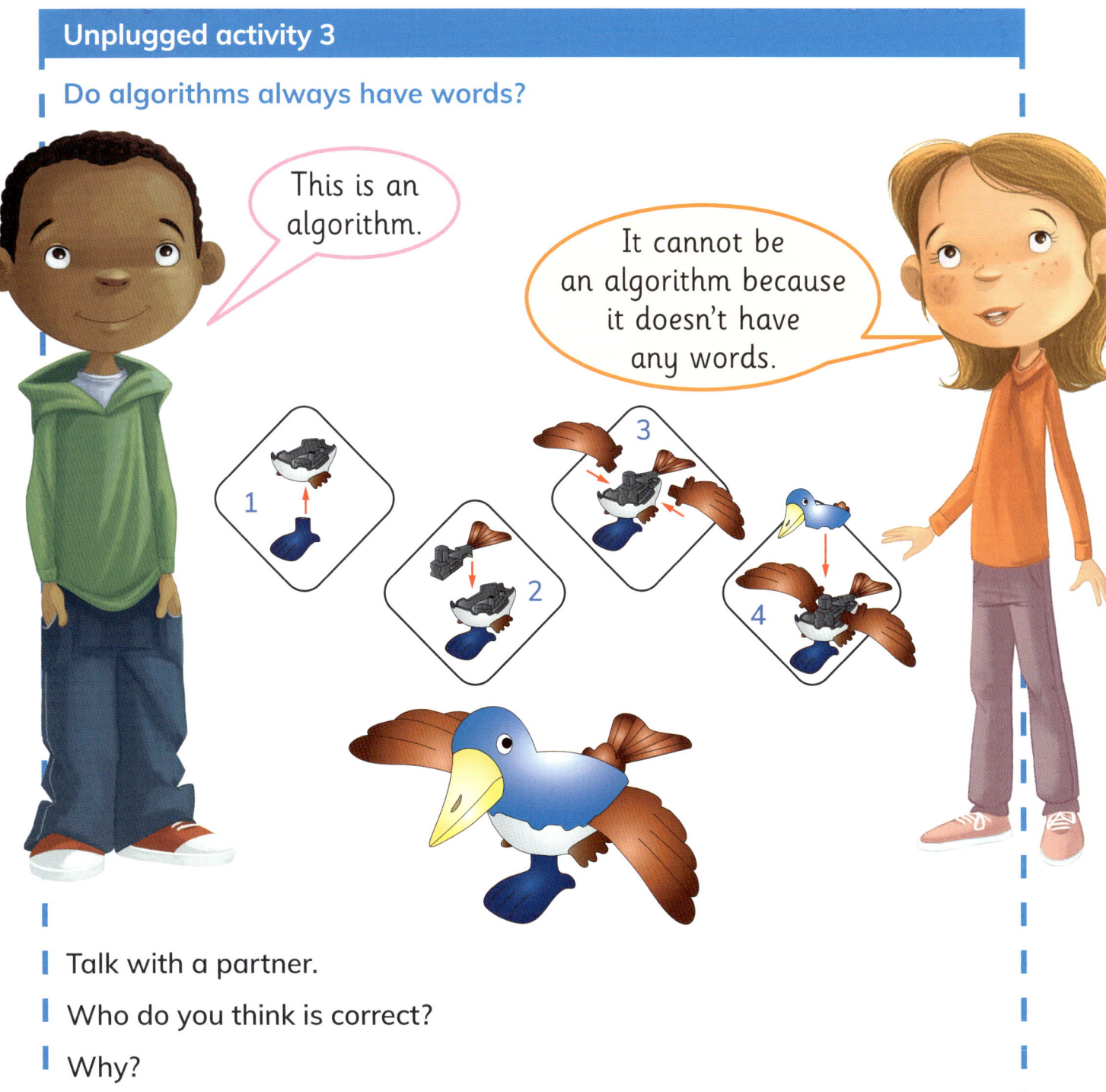

"This is an algorithm."

"It cannot be an algorithm because it doesn't have any words."

- Talk with a partner.
- Who do you think is correct?
- Why?

1 Computational thinking and programming

Unplugged activity 4

What am I drawing?

> You will need:
> a pencil and paper, or a whiteboard pen and mini whiteboard

Marcus wrote an algorithm to draw a picture.

Follow my algorithm to draw a picture!

1. Draw a big square.

   square

2. Draw a large triangle on top of the square. It should sit on top like a hat!

   triangle

3. Draw a rectangle in the middle of the big square.

   rectangle

4. Draw two small squares inside the big square. One on the left, one on the right.

   small squares

1. What did you draw?
2. Is this a good algorithm?
   Why or why not?

1.3 What happens next?

Unplugged activity 5

Make an algorithm to draw a picture

> You will need:
> a pencil and paper, or a whiteboard pen and mini whiteboard

Write or say an algorithm to make this picture.

Add numbers to the instructions.

I'm going to start with: 1 Draw a large circle.

1. How many instructions are in your algorithm?
2. Which instruction is first?
3. Why did you put this one first?

Did you know?

Computers do not have brains like humans do.

They cannot work out what they think we mean.

Computers can only follow the instructions we give them.

This is why our instructions need to be clear.

In programming, we create algorithms to tell the computer what to do.

When we program a Bee-Bot, we can write out the algorithm first to help us plan its route.

1 Computational thinking and programming

Programming task 1

Treasure Island

You will need:
a pencil and paper, or a whiteboard pen and mini whiteboard

Look at the map.

Sofia wants to help the Bee-Bot find the treasure. Can you see it?

1.3 What happens next?

Continued

Some of the instructions are missing in Sofia's algorithm.

1. Go forwards ____ step.
2. Turn right.
3. Go forwards ____ steps.
4. Turn ____ .
5. Go ____ ____ steps.

You have reached the treasure!

Can you help her to complete it using the words below?

| left | four | one | forwards | two |

1 Computational thinking and programming

Making code from an algorithm

In Programming task 1, you completed the algorithm.

To program the Bee-Bot, we change the algorithm into code.

We put the code into the Bee-Bot using the command buttons.

When we press GO, we **run** the code.

Running the code means that the Bee-Bot will follow the instructions we gave it.

Do you remember what each command does? Look back at Topic 1.2 for a reminder!

Programming task 2

Move around the island

> You will need:
> a Bee-Bot, a Bee-Bot treasure map grid made from source file **1.2_treasure_map**

Look at the map and algorithm in Programming task 1.

Draw or say the code that will get the Bee-Bot to the treasure.

42

1.3 What happens next?

Continued

Make sure the commands are in the correct order! I think it starts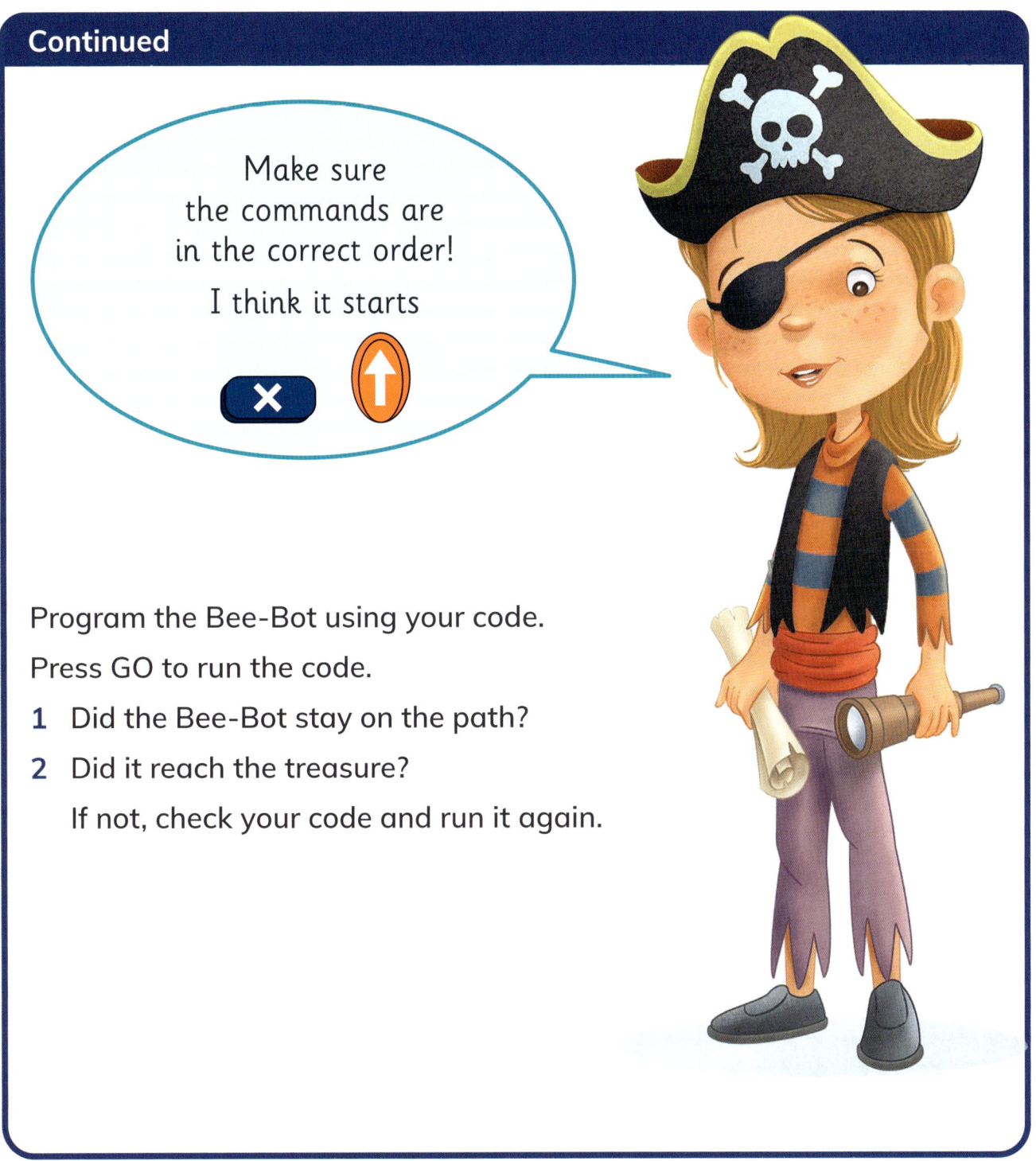

Program the Bee-Bot using your code.

Press GO to run the code.

1. Did the Bee-Bot stay on the path?
2. Did it reach the treasure?

    If not, check your code and run it again.

1 Computational thinking and programming

Programming task 3

Where can we go?

> You will need:
> a Bee-Bot, the Bee-Bot treasure map grid

Help the Bee-Bot to explore the island!

Work with a partner.

1. Change the code so that the Bee-Bot moves:
   - from the start to the shipwreck
   - from the start to the parrots.

   Check the codes using your Bee-Bot.

   The Bee-Bot can also start in a different place.

2. Can you move the Bee-Bot from the monkeys to the waterfall?

1.3 What happens next?

Where is the Bee-Bot going?

Predict means to think about what will happen.

Programming task 4

Predictions

Arun and Zara have written **programs** for their Bee-Bots.

A program is a list of instructions. The instructions make a computer do a task.

Look at the programs on the next page and predict where the Bee-Bots will finish.

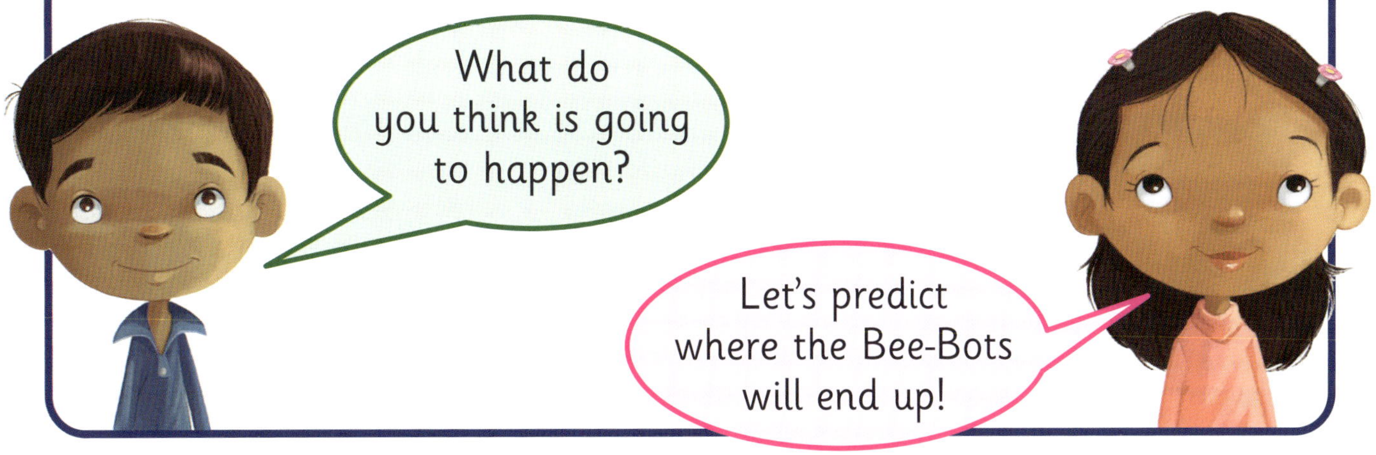

What do you think is going to happen?

Let's predict where the Bee-Bots will end up!

45

1 Computational thinking and programming

Continued

Arun's program

The Bee-Bot is starting at the shipwreck, facing the path.

Continued

Zara's program

The Bee-Bot is starting at the parrots, facing the path.

1 Computational thinking and programming

> **Continued**
>
> **How are we doing?**
>
> Share your predictions with a partner.
>
> Did you get the same answers?
>
> What was easy about the activity? What was difficult?

Questions

1. A Bee-Bot turns in quarter turns.

   Zara wants the Bee-Bot to spin all the way around.

   Help her to program the Bee-Bot.

   How many turns will she need?

2. Marcus forgot to press X at the start of a program.

   What will happen?

> We have looked at different algorithms.
> Some used words. Some used pictures.
> Which type do you like best? Why?

Look what I can do!

- ☐ I can write or draw instructions to build a brick tower.
- ☐ I can write instructions in the correct order.
- ☐ I can make changes to algorithms.
- ☐ I can predict what programs will do.

1.4 Spot the bug

We are going to:
- find out about debugging
- look for errors in programs
- run a program to check it works properly
- look at why a program doesn't always work.

algorithm   error
bug   program
command   run
debugging

1 Computational thinking and programming

Getting started

What do you already know?

- Mistakes are called errors in computing.
- You can write an algorithm for a Bee-Bot and program a Bee-Bot.

Now try this!

Look at these instructions.

The instructions are in the wrong order.

a Put on my shoes

b Go to school

c Get my bag

d Wake up and get out of bed

1.4 Spot the bug

Continued

e Eat breakfast

f Get dressed

g Brush my teeth

1 The first instruction is **d Wake up and get out of bed**.

   Which one comes next? Can you help your teacher to put them in the correct order on the board?

2 What is this algorithm for?

Errors in algorithms

In Topic 1.1, you learnt that algorithms sometimes contain errors. Those errors have to be found and fixed so that the algorithm works properly.

Sometimes, computer code can have errors in it too.

When there is an error in computer code, the program using the code will not work properly.

1 Computational thinking and programming

What is debugging?

In computing, an error is called a **bug**.

Debugging is when you find the error, or bug, and fix it.

Run the program to check that it works. You have fixed the error!

Programming task 1

There and back again

> You will need:
> pencil and paper, or a whiteboard pen and mini whiteboard, a Bee-Bot

Sofia wants to program the Bee-Bot to:
- move forwards two spaces
- move backwards two spaces

so that it ends up back at her feet.

This is her program:

Can you spot the bug?

What does she need to do to make the program work correctly?

Write out the correct instructions.

1.4 Spot the bug

Programming task 2

Fix the driving program

> You will need:
> a pencil and paper, or a whiteboard pen and mini whiteboard, a Bee-Bot, a Bee-Bot racing track grid made from source file **1.3_racing_track**

Here is a driving track.

Zara has written a program to move the Bee-Bot from the start line to the finish line.

Oh no! I've checked it and I think there are too many instructions.

Help Zara to debug the program.

1 Find the error in the program.

   Write it down or say it.

2 Fix the error.

   Write or say the correct program.

53

1 Computational thinking and programming

Continued

3   Program the Bee-Bot.

Run the program to check that you have fixed the error.

How are we doing?

Compare your answers with a partner.

Did you both find the same error?

Tell each other how you worked out what the error was.

Did you know?

We know that in computing, an error is called a bug.

We don't usually see real bugs in computers.

However, in 1947 computer programmers found a moth in a computer.

It was probably the first real bug to stop a computer from working!

1.4 Spot the bug

Programming task 3

Make the Bee-Bot turn all the way around

You will need:
a pencil and paper, or a whiteboard pen and mini whiteboard,
a Bee-Bot

I have made a program. The Bee-Bot should turn all the way around.

The program has a bug. Let's debug it!

1 Help Arun debug his program.

   Write or say the correct program.

   Remember, debugging is when you find the error, or bug, and fix it!

2 Now test the program on your Bee-Bot.

   Does it turn all the way around?

1 Computational thinking and programming

Finding and fixing errors is an important skill. We find and fix mistakes all the time!

Think of other times when you debug your work. Can you think of any times in maths or science? Talk with a partner and share your ideas.

When I write, I check that my sentences start with capital letters and end with full stops.

I check my Bee-Bot programs for bugs!

Look what I can do!

- ☐ I know what debugging is.
- ☐ I can look for errors in programs.
- ☐ I can run a program to check it works properly.
- ☐ I can find why a program doesn't always work.

1.4 Spot the bug

Project

Command the Bee-Bot!

> You will need:
> a small object (like a toy, LEGO brick or pencil), tape or a ruler

1. Find a space.

   Hide a small object a short distance away from you.

   Put something at your feet to mark the start point, like some tape or a ruler.

   Draw or write the path from the start point to the object.

   Use the commands that a Bee-Bot uses:
   - clear
   - forwards
   - backwards
   - left
   - right
   - pause
   - go.

2. Give the algorithm to a partner.

   Can they find the hidden object?

1 Computational thinking and programming

Continued

3. Did the algorithm work?

   If not, look at your algorithm to find the error.

   Fix the error. Ask your partner to try the algorithm again.

4. When you are both happy with your algorithms, give them to another pair.

   Can they can find your hidden objects?

Check your progress

1. What is your favourite snack?

   Think of what you do to make the snack.
   Draw or write the instructions in the correct order.

> My favourite snack is carrots and hummus.
> 1. I put the hummus in a bowl.
> 2. I get carrots out of a bag.
> 3. I dip a carrot in the hummus.
> 4. I put it in my mouth!

2. Marcus predicted what this Bee-Bot code will do:

> I predict that the Bee-Bot will move forwards one step.

Continued

Predict what will happen when you program these commands into a Bee-Bot.

3 Which commands are used in every Bee-Bot sequence?

4 Draw the Bee-Bot commands that make the Bee-Bot move in these ways:

   a Move forwards three steps and turn right.

   b Turn right and then turn left.

   c Move forwards one step, backwards one step, then turn right.

5 Why does Marcus need to debug his program? Choose the correct answer.

   A It works correctly.

   B It doesn't work correctly.

   C He wants to make it longer.

2 Managing data

> 2.1 Using data

We are going to:
- find out how we can use computers to answer different questions
- learn about data and tables
- understand that computers can help to sort and organise data.

> data sort
> personal data table

Getting started

What do you already know?
- Asking questions can help you learn new things.
- There are different ways of finding answers to our questions.
- You can put objects into groups.

Continued

Now try this!

Work with a partner.

Ask your partner a question that helps you learn something new.

Here are two questions you can ask:
- What is your favourite toy?
- Do you have any brothers or sisters?

Write or draw their answer.

What new thing have you learnt?

2 Managing data

Answering questions

We use computers in different ways.

Sometimes we use computers to help us answer questions.

There are lots of ways we can use computers to answer questions.

We can read a website.

2.1 Using data

We can look at tables.

We can watch videos.

We can talk to people.

63

2 Managing data

Unplugged activity 1

Matching game

Zara is going to a park on Saturday.

She is using a computer to find the answers to these questions.

1 What time does the park open?

2 What is the best way to get to the park?

3 What will the weather be like?

4 What is the best thing to do at the park?

Help your teacher to match each question to a computer screen.

A

B
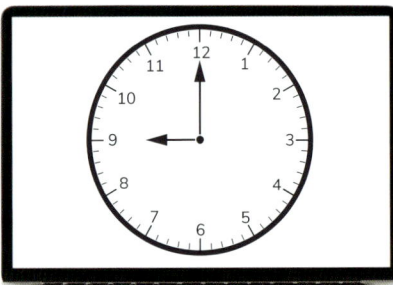

C

D

2.1 Using data

Using computers to answer questions can be helpful.
If you know what the weather is going to be like,
you can decide what activity to do.

Activity 2

What will the weather be like tomorrow?

> You will need:
> a desktop computer, laptop or tablet with internet access,
> website link from your teacher or the Digital Learner's Book

You will use a computer to answer this question:

What will the weather be like tomorrow?

Write or draw your answer.

How are we doing?

Talk to a partner.

Think of another question you could answer using a computer.

65

2 Managing data

What is data?

Look at the table.

A table has headings.

This table has three headings. What are they?

Name	Favourite colour	Favourite animal
Marcus	green	duck

The headings here have a blue background. They are at the top and tell us what is in the table.

Marcus's favourite things are in a row.
A row is a line of things going across the table.

A table shows us data about different things.

A piece of data is a fact. It can be a word, number or picture.

My favourite colour is green.
My favourite animal is a duck.

2.1 Using data

Putting data in a table

Sofia has added data to the table.

Her answers are the data.

Name	Favourite colour	Favourite animal
Marcus	green	duck
Sofia	blue	horse

Putting data in a table makes it easier to see the data.

It is easier to answer questions about the data.

> **Stay safe!**
>
> **Personal data** is about you.
>
> Personal data includes your name, your age and where you live.
>
> You should not share personal data with people you do not know.

2 Managing data

Unplugged activity 3

What is your favourite?

> You will need:
> a pencil and paper, or a whiteboard pen and mini whiteboard

How would you answer the questions Sofia and Marcus answered?

Name	Favourite colour	Favourite animal
1	2	3

If the row is about you, what would you put under each heading?

Write or draw your answers.

Next, share your answers with a partner.

What is their favourite colour?

Is their favourite animal the same as your favourite animal?

2.1 Using data

Computers help us put data in a table

You can use a computer to put data in a table.

A computer can keep lots of data in a table.

> **Practical task 1**
>
> **Add your data**
>
> You will need:
> a desktop computer or laptop with internet access,
> source file **2.1_favourites_table**
>
> Your teacher will give you a file.
>
> 1 Add the data about your favourite colour and favourite animal to the table.
>
> 2 Use the mouse or arrow keys to move to the correct place in the table.
>
> 3 Type your data.
>
> **How are we doing?**
>
> Talk to a partner.
>
> Why is putting data in a table useful?

2 Managing data

You have just completed a practical task.
This is a task you have to do yourself!
Do you think this helps you to learn?
Do you like practical tasks? Why or why not?

Sorting data

Arun visits a farm. He sees four different animals on the farm: sheep, ducks, chickens and horses.

Can you point to one of each type of animal?

2.1 Using data

Arun wants to know which animal is the most common on the farm.

He decides to **sort** the animals into groups.

When we sort, we look for things that are the same.

Arun then organises the data into a table.

Animal	How many?
sheep	7
duck	
chicken	
horse	

There are seven sheep. Do you agree?

2 Managing data

Unplugged activity 4

Sort the animals

Your teacher will copy Arun's table from the last page onto the board.

Can you help them to complete it?

You can do this by sorting the other animals on the farm into groups.

Practical task 2

Table fun!

You will need:
a desktop, laptop or tablet with an internet connection,
a selection of coloured blocks,
source file **2.2_blocks_table**

Your teacher will give you a file for this task.

1. Sort the blocks into different colours.

   How many blocks are there of each colour?

2. Put the data into the table in the file.

   What is the most common colour?

When we sort, we look for things that are the same.

72

Computers help us sort and organise data

Shops use computers to sort and organise the things we buy.

Computers at the checkout count the number of each item.

Using a computer to organise data is much quicker than sorting and organising the data ourselves.

Computers are used in school to sort and organise data.

They help the school know how many pupils are in.

This helps the cooks in the kitchen make the right number of meals.

It would take a long time to count all the things that we buy at the supermarket!

2 Managing data

> **Did you know?**
>
> Computers are used to sort letters.
>
> The letters are sorted into groups of addresses near each other.

Look what I can do!

- ☐ I know that computers can be used in different ways to answer questions.
- ☐ I know how data can be put into tables.
- ☐ I can answer questions using data in tables.
- ☐ I can sort and organise data.
- ☐ I know that computers can sort and organise data.

2.2 Collecting data

We are going to:
- use a form to collect data
- enter data into a computer
- select questions that you can ask to collect data
- select which questions you can answer from your data.

> collect   list
> data   personal data
> form   sort

Getting started

What do you already know?
- We can use data to answer questions.
- Data can be put in tables using a computer.
- Computers can be used to sort and organise data.

2 Managing data

> **Continued**
>
> **Now try this!**
>
> | Animal | Patterned skin/fur? |
> |--------|---------------------|
> | rhino | no |
> | elephant | ? |
> | giraffe | yes |
> | zebra | yes |
>
> Look at the table.
>
> What data completes the table?
>
>
> zebra
>
>
> rhino
>
>
> elephant
>
> giraffe

Computers help us **collect** data.

Collecting data means gathering the data that is needed.

One way to collect data is to use a **form**.

A form has questions for people to answer.

We do not need to speak to people to collect their answers.

We can send the questions to people all over the world.

Talk to a partner.

2.2 Collecting data

What question would you ask your family members using a form?

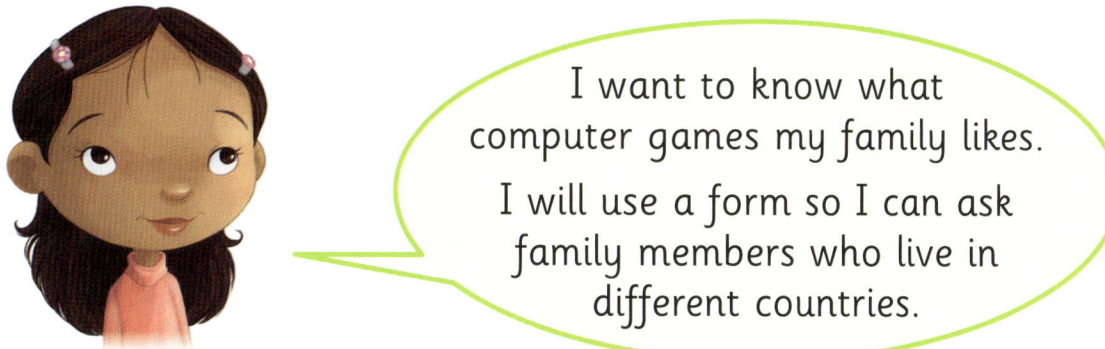

I want to know what computer games my family likes.
I will use a form so I can ask family members who live in different countries.

Sometimes a form uses a *list* to help people answer a question.

A list is a set of answers to a question.

The person clicks on an answer from the list to answer the question.

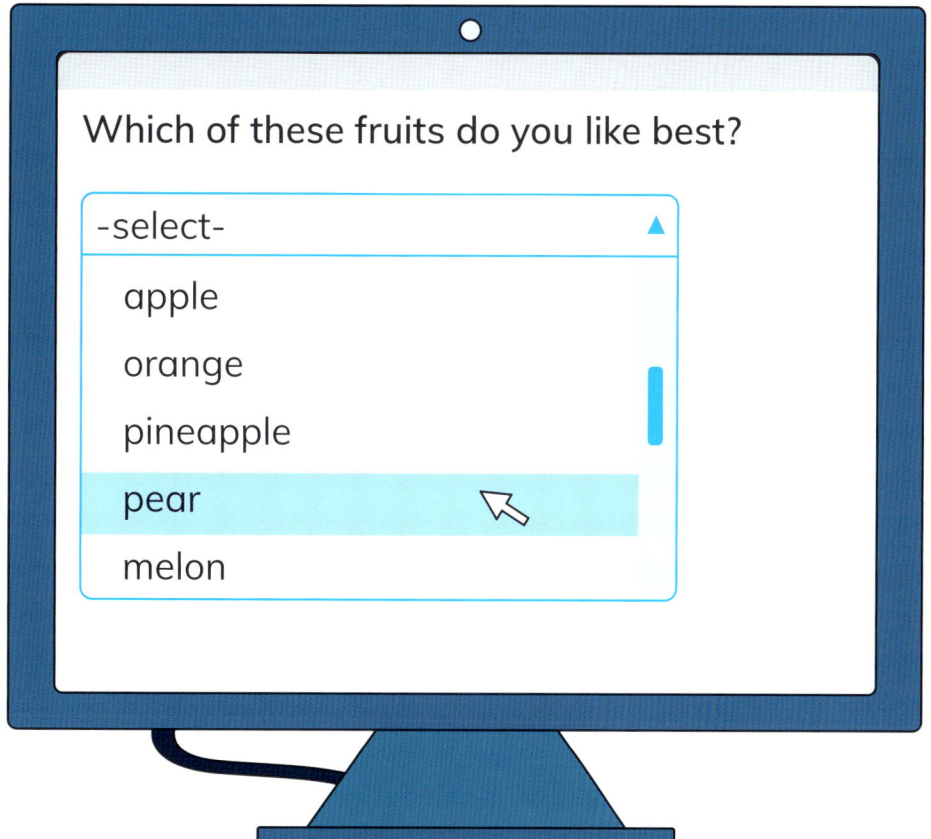

77

2 Managing data

Answering questions using a form

Arun is using a form to help him answer a question.

There are four types of stories that I like. It's hard to decide what my favourite type is! I wonder what type of book my classmates like best?

The form will collect the data.

Arun can use this data to answer his question.

Arun is going to use a list in his form.

Questions

1 Which question should Arun put on his form? Choose the correct answer.

   A Which lesson do you prefer?

   B Which type of story do you prefer?

   C Which sport do you prefer?

2 Which list should Arun use to answer his question? Choose the correct answer.

   A athletics, cricket, running, swimming

   B adventure stories, animal stories, funny stories, space stories

   C art, computing, maths, science

2.2 Collecting data

Activity 1

Fill out the form

> You will need:
> a desktop computer, laptop or tablet with internet access, online form **2.3_stories_form**

Your teacher will give you Arun's form.

Sofia was not in school when Arun collected the data.

Add Sofia's name and answer to the form.

I prefer space stories.

2 Managing data

Arun collects the data from his classmates.

Most of his classmates prefer to read adventure stories.

Stay safe!

If a form asks for personal data like your full name, address or telephone number, tell a trusted adult straight away.

Did you know?

We can help to collect data for scientists.

Here is some data that we can collect:

- We can count the birds we see on a certain day.
- We can count the cars in our street.
- We can count the types of shops in our town.

Then we can enter the data on a form.

Scientists can use the collected data to answer their questions.

2.2 Collecting data

Ask the right question

We need to ask the right question to get the right data.

Zara wants to find out which of her friends like cricket. It is her favourite sport.

She asks her friends a question.

What is your favourite sport?

She puts the data in a table.

Name	Favourite sport
Zara	cricket
Arun	swimming
Sofia	running
Marcus	swimming

Can Zara use the data in the table to answer the question 'Who likes cricket?'

2 Managing data

Zara asked the wrong question.

Her friends may like cricket even if it is not their favourite sport.

Zara tried a different question. She asked 'Do you like cricket?'

2.2 Collecting data

Questions

3 Which question should Marcus ask to collect the right data?

   A What is your favourite cartoon character?

   B What is your favourite television programme?

   C Do you like watching cartoons?

I want to know which of my friends like watching cartoons.

4 Sofia wants to know which of her friends like playing computer games.

   What question should she ask?

When you are collecting data, how do you know the right question to ask?

Share ideas with a partner.

2 Managing data

Unplugged activity 2

Which questions can I answer?

I am going to make fruit kebabs for my friends. I am going to use a form to find out which fruits they want.

Question 1: What is your name?

Marcus

Question 2 Which three fruits would you like on your fruit kebab?

- mango ✓
- melon ✓
- apple ☐
- strawberry ☐
- grapes ✓
- pineapple ☐

Sofia puts the data from the form into a table.

Name	Fruit 1	Fruit 2	Fruit 3
Marcus	mango	grapes	melon
Zara	mango	apple	pineapple
Arun	mango	melon	pineapple

Sofia is using the data to answer questions.

2.2 Collecting data

Continued

How many of these questions can she answer?
Choose the correct answers.

A Which fruits does Arun want on his kebab?

B Who likes vegetables more than fruit?

C How many people want grapes on their kebabs?

Marcus did not choose apples, so he does not like apples.

Is Sofia correct?

The question asked Marcus which fruits he wanted on his kebab.

He did not choose apples, but he might still like them.

How am I doing?

Did you choose the right questions?

How did you work out the questions that Sofia could answer?
Tell your partner.

Look what I can do!

☐ I can use a form to collect and enter data into a computer.

☐ I can select questions to ask when collecting data.

☐ I can select which questions can and cannot be answered from collected data.

2 Managing data

Project

Collect your own data!

> You will need:
> a desktop computer, laptop or tablet with internet access,
> source file **2.4_project_table**

Work with a partner or in small groups.

You are going to collect data from your class to answer a question.

1   Decide what you want to find out.

   You could ask about:

   - drinks
   - books
   - films
   - fruits
   - songs
   - sports

   or you can choose your own idea.

> **Continued**
>
> 2 Collect your data.
>
>   What question are you going to ask?
>
>   Make a list of answers to choose from.
>
>   Have four, five or six answers in your list.
>
>   Ask ten of your classmates the question.
>
> 3 Your teacher will give you a file.
>
>   It has an empty table.
>
>   Put your data in the table.
>
> 4 Now you can use the collected data to answer these questions:
>
>   a Were any choices selected by more than one person?
>
>   b Were any choices selected by only one person?

2 Managing data

Check your progress

1 Arun is using a computer to find the answer to a question.

Which question is he trying to answer?

Choose the correct answer.

A What time does the swimming pool open?

B Will it rain tomorrow?

C How long will it take to cycle to school?

2 Zara used a form to collect data about her classmates' favourite fruit.

Name	Favourite fruit
Arun	apple
Sofia	banana
Marcus	orange
Paulo	apple
Victor	banana
Lucas	banana

Continued

Zara wants to organise the data to see how many classmates chose each fruit.

What are the numbers that complete Zara's table?

Fruit	How many?
orange	1
banana	
apple	

3 a Marcus wants to find out what his family's favourite ice cream is.

He uses a computer to help collect the data.

What else should he use to help collect the data? Choose the correct answer.

A an algorithm

B a form

C a sequence

b Marcus writes a set of answers to select from. What is this called? Choose the correct answer.

A a list

B a choice

C a selection

2 Managing data

Continued

4 Sofia has collected data about her classmates' favourite type of TV programme.

Name	Favourite type of TV programme
Arun	nature
Zara	sports
Marcus	cartoon
Chad	cartoon
Vishni	cartoon
Kamili	nature

sports programmes   nature programmes   cartoon programmes

a Which of these questions can Sofia answer using the data? Choose the correct answers.

Clue: there is more than one question Sofia can answer.

A Which classmates like nature programmes the most?

B What is Chad's favourite type of TV programme?

C Who watched a film last night?

D How many classmates chose cartoons?

b Think of another question that Sofia can answer using the data.

3 > Networks and digital communication

> 3.1 Get connected

We are going to:

- learn that computers can connect to each other to make a network
- identify devices that can be connected to a network
- find out how devices can be connected to a network.

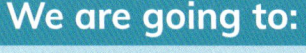

connect
desktop computer
device
laptop computer
network

printer
smartphone
tablet
wi-fi
wireless

3 Networks and digital communication

> **Getting started**
>
> **What do you already know?**
> - There are different types of computers.
> - People use computers in lots of different places, such as at home, work and school.
>
> **Now try this!**
>
> Look at the two computers in the picture.
>
> Talk to a partner.
>
> What is different about the two computers?

Different types of computers

All computers are devices.

Devices are pieces of equipment that do a task or a group of tasks.

You have already learned about some of the tasks that computers can do.

We can use some devices with our computers, such as printers. These devices work with our computers when they are doing their task.

Making a connection

Marcus and Sofia can connect their computers together.

Connect means to join with something else.

When computers or other devices are connected, there is a link between them.

3 Networks and digital communication

What is a network?

Look at these pictures.

desktop computer

laptop

printer

tablet

smartphone

You will learn more about these types of computer in Unit 4!

3.1 Get connected

A **network** can connect all of these computers and devices.

A network is two or more computers that are joined together.

We can share information between computers that are on the same network.

Some devices that we use with computers can also connect to a network.

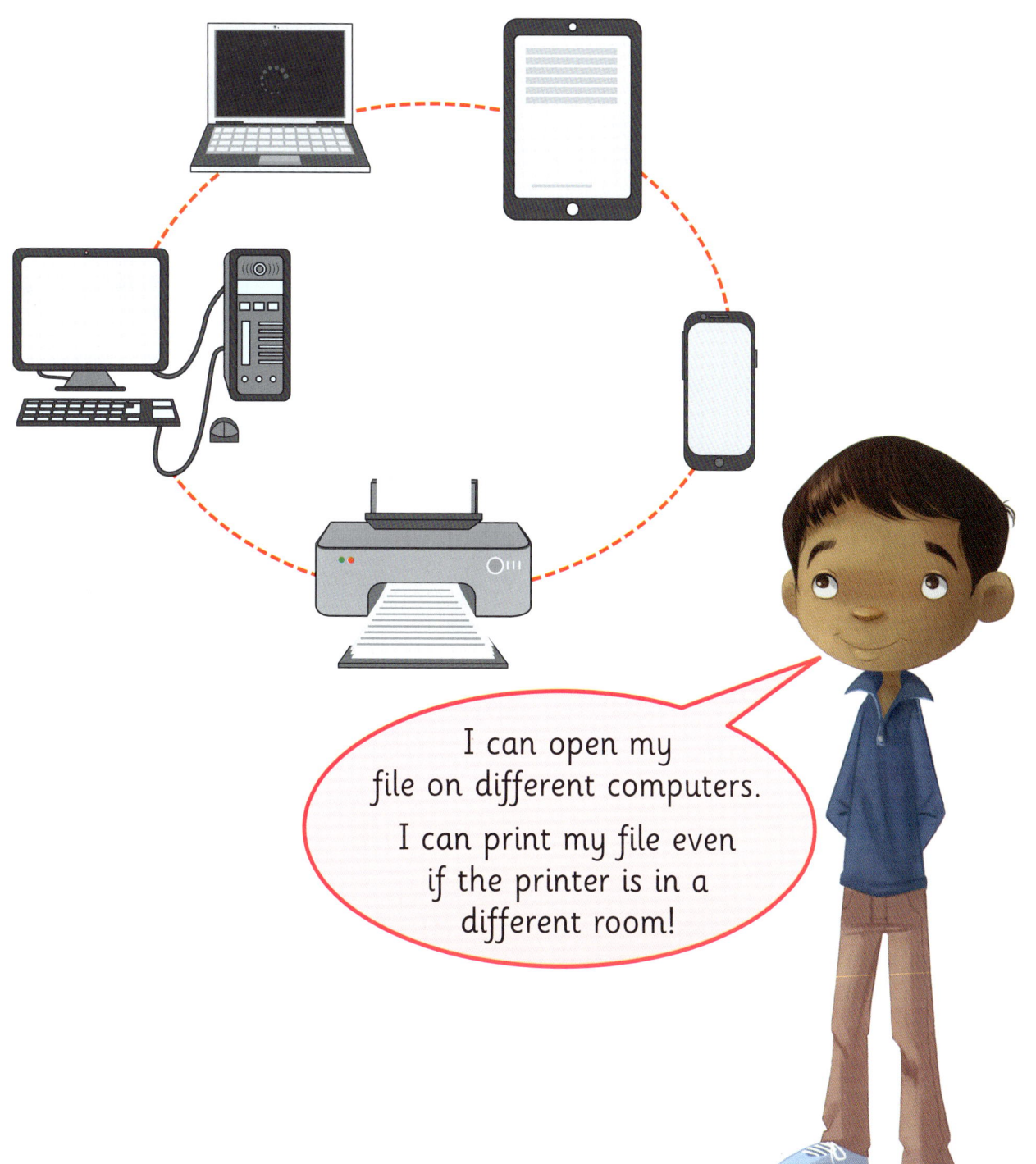

I can open my file on different computers.
I can print my file even if the printer is in a different room!

3 Networks and digital communication

Unplugged activity 1

Can the objects be connected to a network?

You will need:
a pencil and paper, or a whiteboard pen and mini whiteboard

Which of these objects can be connected to a computer network?

Which cannot?

laptop computer

pencil

printer

book

tablet

ruler

A pencil cannot be connected to a network.

3.1 Get connected

> **Did you know?**
>
> The first computer network started in 1969 when four computers were connected together.
>
> The network was called ARPANET.

How do devices connect to a network?

Computers and devices can be connected to networks in different ways.

Some computers and devices can be connected to a network by wires like this.

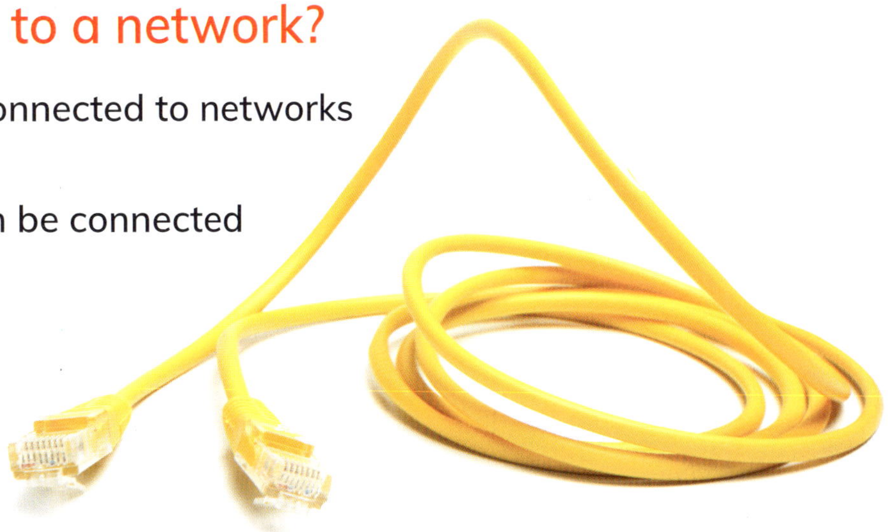

97

3 Networks and digital communication

Other computers and devices make a **wireless** connection to the network.

This means they do not need wires to connect to the network.

The common wireless connection in our homes and school is known as **wi-fi**.

The tablet is connected to the school network. It does not need a wire to connect to the network.

This is the wi-fi sign:

I have seen this sign in the library. Where have you seen it?

98

3.1 Get connected

Unplugged activity 2

How are they connected?

> You will need:
> a pencil and paper, or a whiteboard pen and mini whiteboard

With your teacher, look round your classroom or library.

Find computers and devices (like printers) that are part of your school's network.

- Say the name of each device.
- Draw a picture of each device.
- Does the device use a wire to connect to the network? If it does, put a tick ✓ next to your picture.

How am I doing?

- How many devices were connected by wires?
- How many devices had a wireless connection?

Share your answers with a partner.

Stay safe!

Always ask an adult to help you connect your computer to a new network.

Other computers on the network might be able to see information on your computer.

3 Networks and digital communication

> **Unplugged activity 3**
>
> **Make a network!**
>
> > You will need:
> > a pencil and paper
>
> Your teacher will put you in small groups.
>
> Each of you will be one of these devices. Which do you choose?
>
>
>
> desktop computer   laptop computer   tablet
>
>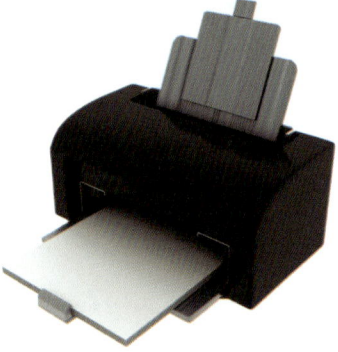
>
> printer   smartphone
>
> 1 Write the name of the device on a piece of paper.
>
> Hold up your piece of paper so that everyone in your group can see it.
>
> Make sure you can see what everyone else has chosen.
>
> Then join hands. You are all part of one network!

3.1 Get connected

> **Continued**
>
> 2. Look at the pictures of the devices again.
>   Does your device use a wire to connect to the network?
>
>   Tell the rest of your group.
>
> 3. Your teacher will give one of the computers the name of an animal.
>
>   That learner will whisper the name to one of the learners next to them – they have sent it to another part of the network!
>
>   When it has gone round the whole network, send it to the printer.
>
>   The learner who is the printer can draw the animal and take it to the teacher! Is it correct?

Do you like learning in a group?
Do you like playing games to learn?

Look what I can do!

- [ ] I know that some devices can connect to each other to make a network.
- [ ] I know that devices connected to the same network can share information.
- [ ] I understand that some devices use wires to connect to a network.
- [ ] I understand that some devices do not need wires to connect to a network.

3 Networks and digital communication

> 3.2 Introducing the internet

We are going to:
- learn that the internet is a network of computers connected around the world
- learn what online and offline mean
- know that there are times when we cannot use the internet.

device
internet
network
offline
online

Getting started

What do you already know?
- You can connect computers together to form a network.
- You can share information between computers that are connected to a network.

Now try this!

Work with a partner.

Talk about the things you like to do on a computer.

I like talking to my grandparents. They live in a different country.

I like watching videos.

I like finding out about my favourite sports star.

I like playing computer games with my friends.

3.2 Introducing the internet

What is the internet?

In Topic 3.1 we learnt that a network is two or more computers that are joined together.

We can share information between the computers.

Arun can use the internet to share the photo with his grandma.

3 Networks and digital communication

The internet is a network of many computers connected together across the world.

When you are connected to the internet, you can share information with other people around the world.

You can use the internet to:
- learn how to play an instrument
- help you with school work
- watch films
- listen to music.

Stay safe!

You do not know everyone who is on the internet.

Never talk to people who you do not know.

Tell an adult when you see or hear something that makes you feel worried or upset.

Unplugged activity 1

Do you need the internet?

Look at these activities.

Talk to a friend in a different country

Eat lunch

Find out about a famous person

Check the weather forecast

Go swimming

Point to each activity.

Do you need the internet to do the activity?

How am I doing?

- Did you know which activities need the internet?

  Draw a smiley face in your notebook.

- If you are not sure, talk to someone who has drawn a smiley face in their notebook.

  How did they decide?

3 Networks and digital communication

Did you know?

Information shared over the internet travels through wires at the bottom of the sea.

This allows the information to travel from one area of the world to another.

You have learnt about different ways that people use the internet.

Think of one way you use the internet.

Why do you need the internet to do this activity?

Stay safe!

Make sure a trusted adult knows what you are doing when you are on the internet.

They will be able to check that it is safe.

Online and offline

When we are connected to the internet, we are online.

We can share information with other people who are online.

When we are not connected to the internet, we are offline.

We cannot use the internet.

We cannot share information with other people.

Who can Sofia play with?

3 Networks and digital communication

Unplugged activity 2

Online or offline?

Look at the pictures of Farah.

Is she online or offline in each picture?

When the internet is not available

Sometimes we are offline because we want to be.

Sometimes we are offline because we cannot connect to the internet. The internet is not available.

> I am offline because I am taking a break from using the internet.

> I am offline because I cannot connect my device to the internet.

When we cannot connect to the internet, we cannot share information with other computers.

When the internet is not available, we can try to fix the problem with a trusted adult.

Sometimes we need to wait for the problem to be fixed.

3.2 Introducing the internet

Unplugged activity 3

Offline time

> You will need:
> a pencil and paper, or
> a whiteboard pen and
> mini whiteboard

Talk to a partner. When did you want to use the internet but it wasn't working?

Draw a picture of something you enjoy doing that does not need the internet.

Did you know?

We do not always need to be connected to the internet when we are using computer devices.

We can do things like write a story on a computer when the internet is not available.

Look what I can do!

- [ ] I know that the internet is a network of computers connected around the world.
- [ ] I understand what online and offline mean.
- [ ] I understand that there are times when the internet is not available.

3 Networks and digital communication

Project

Our favourite activities

You will need:
paper and coloured pens or pencils

> I like cooking with Dad. This is an offline activity. I do not need the internet to cook.

As a class, talk about online and offline activities.

What is the difference between them?

Work with a partner.

Make a poster to show activities that you like to do online and activities that you like to do offline. You can write or draw the activities.

Which group of activities can you do if the internet is not available?

> My mum and I like to video call my uncle. This is an online activity. We need the internet to talk to someone who lives in a different country.

What we like to do!

Offline	Online

110

3.2 Introducing the internet

Check your progress

1 Zara, Marcus and Sofia have connected their computers together.

   What is the name for a group of computers that are connected? Choose the correct answer.

   A set

   B group

   C network

2 Arun wants to connect to the same network as his friends.

   Which objects can he use to connect to the network?

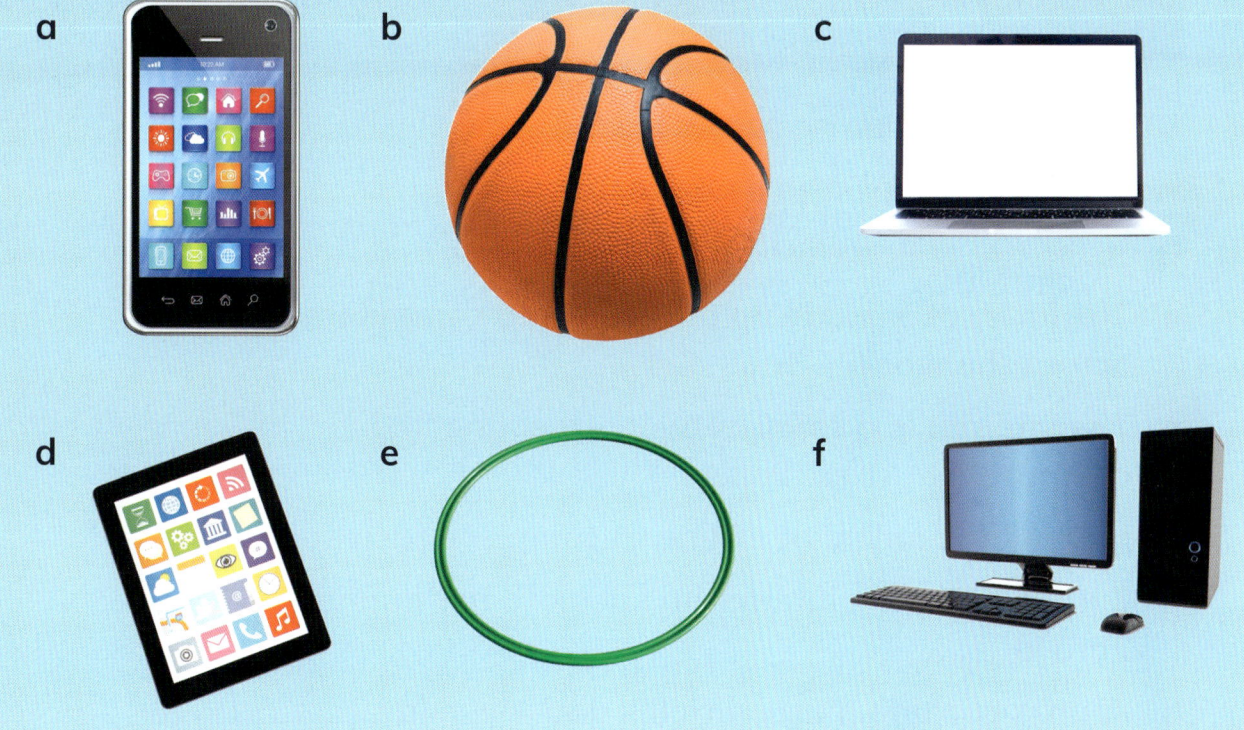

111

3 Networks and digital communication

Continued

3 Some computers use a wire to connect to a network.

Other computers do not use a wire.

How do they connect to a network?

4 Choose True or False for each sentence.

a The internet is made up of connected computers across the world.   True   False

b The internet is a small network of connected computers.   True   False

5 Use the words **online** or **offline** to complete each sentence.

a Zara is using the internet to speak to her auntie. Zara is _____.

b Arun is cooking pizza with his dad. Arun is _____.

c Marcus's mum is using her phone to look up directions to the cinema. She is _____.

4 Computer systems

> 4.1 Types of technology

We are going to:

- name different types of computers
- find out how we use computers for different things
- understand that computers can run programs or apps.

> app laptop computer
> desktop computer smartphone
> games console tablet

Getting started

What do you already know?

- You see different types of computers at home and school.
- You use computers to do schoolwork, watch videos or play games.

4 Computer systems

> **Continued**
>
> **Now try this!**
>
> What computers can you see? How are they different to each other?

Different types of computer

There are many different types of computer. There are:

- desktop computers

    Desktop computers are not easy to carry around. They usually have a separate screen, keyboard and mouse. They would not fit in your bag!

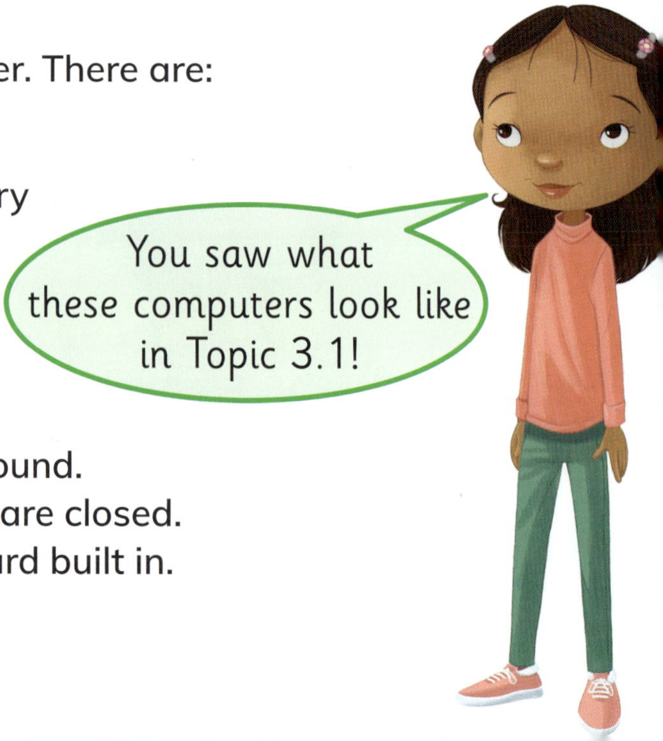

- laptop computers

    Laptop computers are easy to carry around. They have a lid and are flat when they are closed. They have a screen, mouse and keyboard built in.

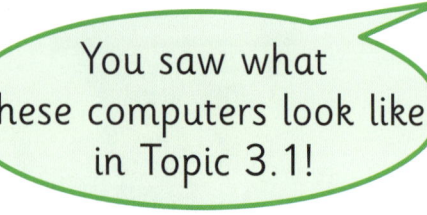

You saw what these computers look like in Topic 3.1!

4.1 Types of technology

- tablets

  Tablets are even easier to carry around than laptops. You can use your hands to click and type!

- smartphones

  These are phones that can be carried around and used like a computer.

- **games consoles**

  Games consoles are computers that are mainly used for playing fun games!

Unplugged activity 1

Find the computers

Work with a partner.

There are five types of computer in the picture.

Marcus has a games console to play games.

1. Find the other four types of computer.

   Try to name them.

2. What can each type of computer be used for?

3. How many of these types of computer have you used before? Tell a partner.

Stay safe!

Marcus uses computers in the living room of his house.

His family are near him to see and hear what he is doing.

They help him stay safe.

4 Computer systems

Using computers for different tasks

We use different types of computers to do different tasks.

We can:

- play games

- talk to friends and family

- do schoolwork

- watch videos.

You can use computers to do other tasks too!

4.1 Types of technology

Unplugged activity 2

Computer hunt!

> **You will need:**
> a pencil and paper, or a whiteboard pen and mini whiteboard

With your teacher, visit different parts of the school.

Look for people using computers.

Ask five people what they are using a computer for.

As a class, make a list of what the computers are being used for.

How am I doing?

Can you remember what people use computers for?

Draw a smiley face on the list for each task that you remember.

How many smiley faces can you get?

4 Computer systems

What are apps and programs?

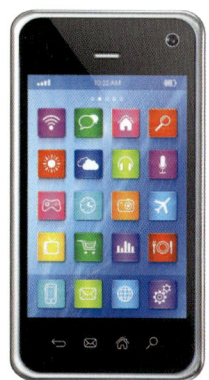

Smartphones have **apps**.

Tablets have apps.

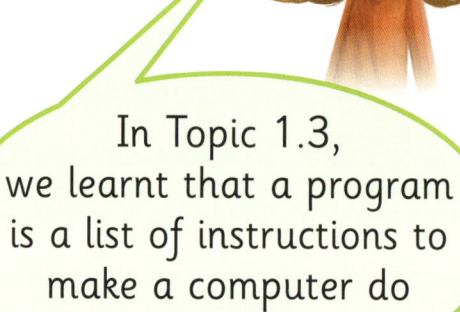

Apps are the same as programs on a laptop or desktop computer.

Computers can run programs and apps.

In Topic 1.3, we learnt that a program is a list of instructions to make a computer do a task.

4.1 Types of technology

Apps and programs help us to do lots of different things.

We can play games.

We can collect data.

In Topic 1.3, we learnt that when a program is run, the computer follows the instructions we gave it.

Unplugged activity 3

Which apps?

Zara has homework. She needs to:
- find out about a famous person
- write about the person's life
- draw the person.

Zara has six different apps on her tablet.

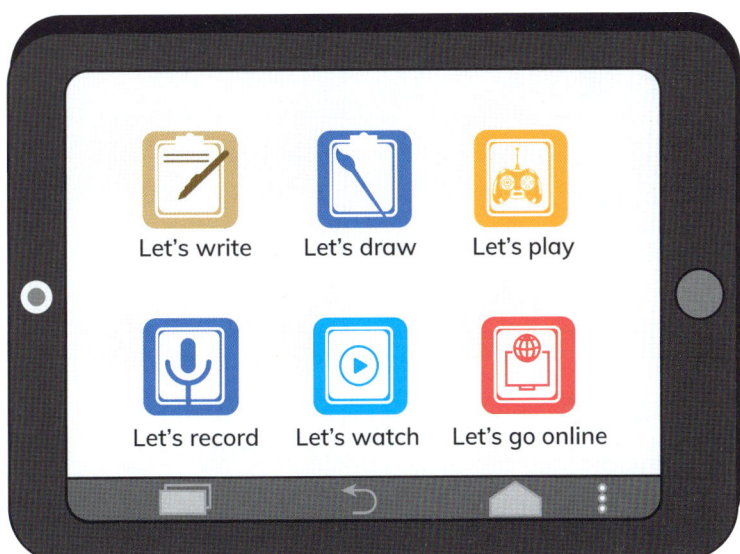

Talk to a partner.

Can Zara use the same app for all of her homework?

Which app should Zara use for each task?

119

4 Computer systems

Question

1. What have you used an app or program for?

   Try to think of four (or more!) things.

   Tell a partner. Did they think of different things than you?

> **Activity 4**
>
> **App hunt!**
>
> > You will need:
> > a tablet with apps, or a laptop or desktop computer with programs
>
> Here are four types of app or program that you might find on a tablet, laptop or desktop computer.
>
> | Type of app or program | What you can do |
> |---|---|
> | Communication | Talk with other people using text, voice audio or video. |
> | Entertainment | Play games, read books, watch videos, listen to music and more. |
> | Creativity | Make pictures, presentations, documents, videos, animations and more. |
> | Research | Learn more about people and things. |

4.1 Types of technology

Continued

Work with a partner.

Look at the apps or programs on your computer.

How many are there?

Are there too many to count?

Find one app or program of each type given in the table.

Open and explore the apps or programs.

Say the name of the app or program you find for each type.

Did you know?

There are millions of different apps for tablets!

4 Computer systems

Unplugged activity 5

My app idea

> You will need:
> paper, pencils and coloured pencils

Think of an idea for an app.

Draw a picture to show what your app is about.

Say the things you can do with the app.

My app is about football players. You can find out how many goals they have scored.

My app helps you draw birthday cards for your friends and family.

How are we doing?

Work in a small group.

Take turns to share your idea for an app.

Sort the apps into the four types we looked at in Activity 4.

Are there any apps that do not fit into one of the four types?

4.1 Types of technology

How does working in a group help you to learn?
What do you do when others in the group have different ideas?

Look what I can do!

- ☐ I can name different types of computer.
- ☐ I know that computers do different things.
- ☐ I understand that computers run different types of apps and programs.

4 Computer systems

> 4.2 Ins and outs

We are going to:
- learn different ways to get information into computers
- learn how we get information from computers.

information   output
input   speakers
keyboard   touchscreen
mouse

Getting started

What do you already know?
- You have learnt about different types of computers.
- You may have heard sound coming from a computer's speakers.
- You may have typed words using a keyboard.

Now try this!

How did you last use a computer?

Did you use a mouse and keyboard? Did you touch the screen?

Tell a partner.

4.2 Ins and outs

The mouse and keyboard

You learnt about different types of computers in Topic 4.1.

We use different types of computers in different ways.

Look at the photo.
Talk with a partner.

Can you point to the mouse and the keyboard?

You need a **mouse** and **keyboard** to use a desktop computer.

> A keyboard is a set of keys that you press to type words and numbers into a computer.

> You move the mouse and press the buttons to use the computer.

125

4 Computer systems

The mouse and keyboard send **information** into the computer.

They **input** information.

The computer uses this information.

Stay safe!

Zara always checks which websites she is allowed to go on.

She only goes online with a trusted adult.

I can type the name of the cartoon I want to watch using the keyboard. I can use the mouse to click on the video to start it.

Unplugged activity 1

Selfie

You will need:
coloured pencils and paper, or a whiteboard pen and mini whiteboard

Draw a picture of yourself using a computer.

Share your picture with the class.

How do you use the computer you have drawn?

4.2 Ins and outs

The touchscreen

Did anyone draw themselves using a tablet or smartphone in Unplugged activity 1?

We do not usually use a mouse and keyboard with a smartphone or tablet.

What do we use instead?

Smartphones and tablets have a **touchscreen**.

We touch the screen to send information to the computer.

We can tap the screen to input letters.

We can tap the screen to input information.

Some laptops have a touchscreen too.

4 Computer systems

Unplugged activity 2

Same and different

The children are using a desktop computer, a tablet and a laptop.

They are using the computers in different ways.

Talk to a partner.

What is different about the way the children are using the desktop computer and the tablet?

What is the same about the way the children are using the desktop computer and the laptop?

4.2 Ins and outs

Did you know?

There are lots of ways to use a computer.

This person is using a sip and puff tube.

This child is using a tracker ball.

4 Computer systems

Activity 3

Logging in

> You will need:
> a school computer or tablet

Visit your school's website or open an app using a school computer or tablet.

Which of these devices did you use?

- A mouse
- A keyboard
- A touchscreen

Or did you use something else?

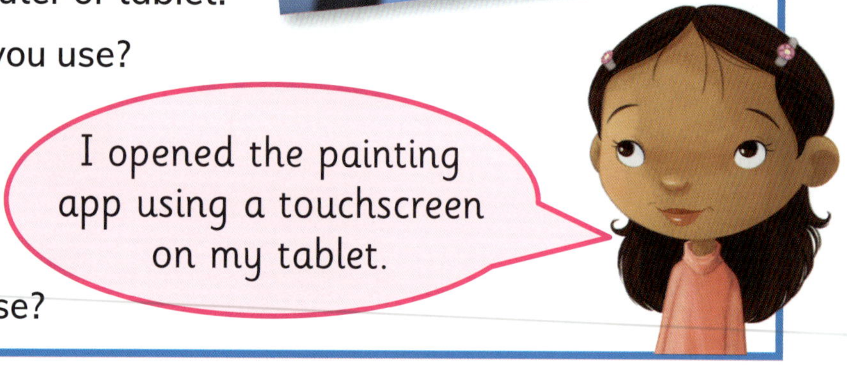

"I opened the painting app using a touchscreen on my tablet."

4.2 Ins and outs

Unplugged activity 4

How many?

> You will need:
> a pencil and paper

For a week, write or draw:
- the different types of computers you use
- the different ways you use each computer.

At the end of the week, talk to a partner.

How many different types of computers did you use?

How many different ways did you input information into the computers?

How are we doing?

List the different ways that you can use a computer.

Compare your list with a partner.

How are your lists different?

Did it get easier to name and remember the different ways you use computers?

Why does doing something for a long time like a week help us to remember better?

4 Computer systems

Speakers

Computers also **output** information to us.

They let us hear and see things.

Look at the picture.

Point to the device that lets us hear music from the computer.

Speakers output information.

They help us hear music.

They help us hear the sound from videos.

Computer screens

Computers output information to us in other ways.

A screen outputs information from a computer.

Questions

Sofia and Marcus are using a desktop computer to create a drawing.

1. What is Marcus using to input information into the computer?
2. What part of the computer outputs information so that we can see the drawing?

4.2 Ins and outs

Unplugged activity 5

Which way?

We have learnt how we input information to computers and how they output information.

Remember:

- **input** – information goes **into** the computer
- **output** – information comes **out of** the computer.

Work with a partner. For each sentence below, think about:

Is the information going into the computer or coming out of it?

Write or say **input** if it is going into the computer.

Write or say **output** if it is coming out of it.

1   Ana is listening to music from her computer speakers.

2   Miguel is watching a video on his tablet.

4 Computer systems

Continued

3 Maryam is typing a story using a keyboard.

How are we doing?

Look at the picture with a partner.

Draw a star for anything in the picture that inputs information into the computer.

Draw a smiley face for anything in the picture that outputs information from the computer.

Compare your stars and faces with another pair.

Do you have the same number?

Look what I can do!

☐ I understand different ways to get information into computers.

☐ I understand different ways that computers output information to us.

> 4.3 Bots everywhere!

We are going to:
- learn that many devices are controlled by computers
- identify what robots are and what they can do.

control
device
robot

Getting started

What do you already know?

- A device is a piece of equipment that can do a task or group of tasks.

    Here are some devices that you may have seen in your home:

    - a digital alarm clock
    - a washing machine.
    - a microwave

- You might have some ideas about what a robot is. Share your ideas with a partner.

Now try this!

Traffic lights need to change to green or red at the right time to stop cars crashing into each other!

Talk to a partner. How do you think a traffic light knows when to change colour?

4 Computer systems

How does it work?

Many devices use special computers to **control** what they do.

Control means getting something to do what you want.

The special computer helps the device to work.

Arun's digital alarm clock has a small computer in it.

The computer lets Arun:

- set the time on the clock
- set an alarm to get up for school
- set a later alarm at the weekend so that he can stay in bed longer!

My alarm clock has a computer in it.

I can set the time for my alarm using the buttons.

Computers that control devices like Arun's alarm clock are different to the computers you learnt about in Topic 4.1.

They can only help with certain tasks.

You can't take the computer out of the clock and play games on it!

4.3 Bots everywhere!

Unplugged activity 1

Matching game

Look at the devices and the list of jobs.

Each device has a computer inside it.

Help your teacher to match each device to its job.

Devices:

1 washing machine

2 microwave

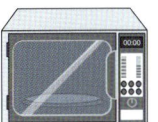

3 traffic lights

4 digital camera

5 vending machine

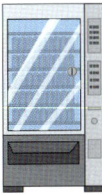

Jobs:

a   Lets you take a picture and look at it.

b   Makes sure the lights come on in the correct order.

c   Heats food for the correct amount of time.

d   Lets you choose and collect a drink.

e   Adds soap and water to clothes and spins to clean them.

4 Computer systems

Do you like to know how things work?
Why or why not?

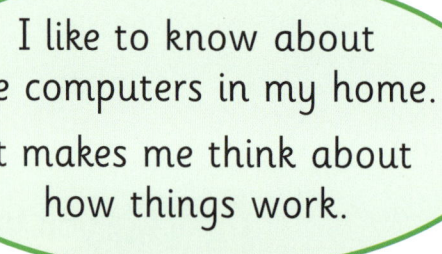

I like to know about the computers in my home. It makes me think about how things work.

Did you know?

Cars have lots of computers inside them.

The computers control different parts of a car.

They make the brakes work.

They make the lights work.

What are robots?

Some devices do difficult jobs with the help of a computer.

They do these jobs on their own, without lots of help from humans.

We call these devices **robots**.

4.3 Bots everywhere!

Real robots in the world

Talk to a partner.

What do you think the robot in the picture might do?

This robot is used for farming.

It moves on its own across fields, looking for weeds.

It then sends another robot out to get rid of the weeds!

4 Computer systems

TV and films often show robots that look like humans, but most robots don't.

Look at this robot vacuum cleaner. It doesn't look like a human!

Look at the robot that the person is wearing.

This special robot helps people walk.

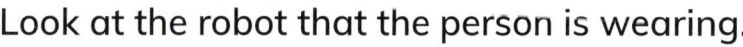

4.3 Bots everywhere!

This is a drone.

Some businesses use drones to deliver things to you.

Did you know?
Self-driving cars are a type of robot too!

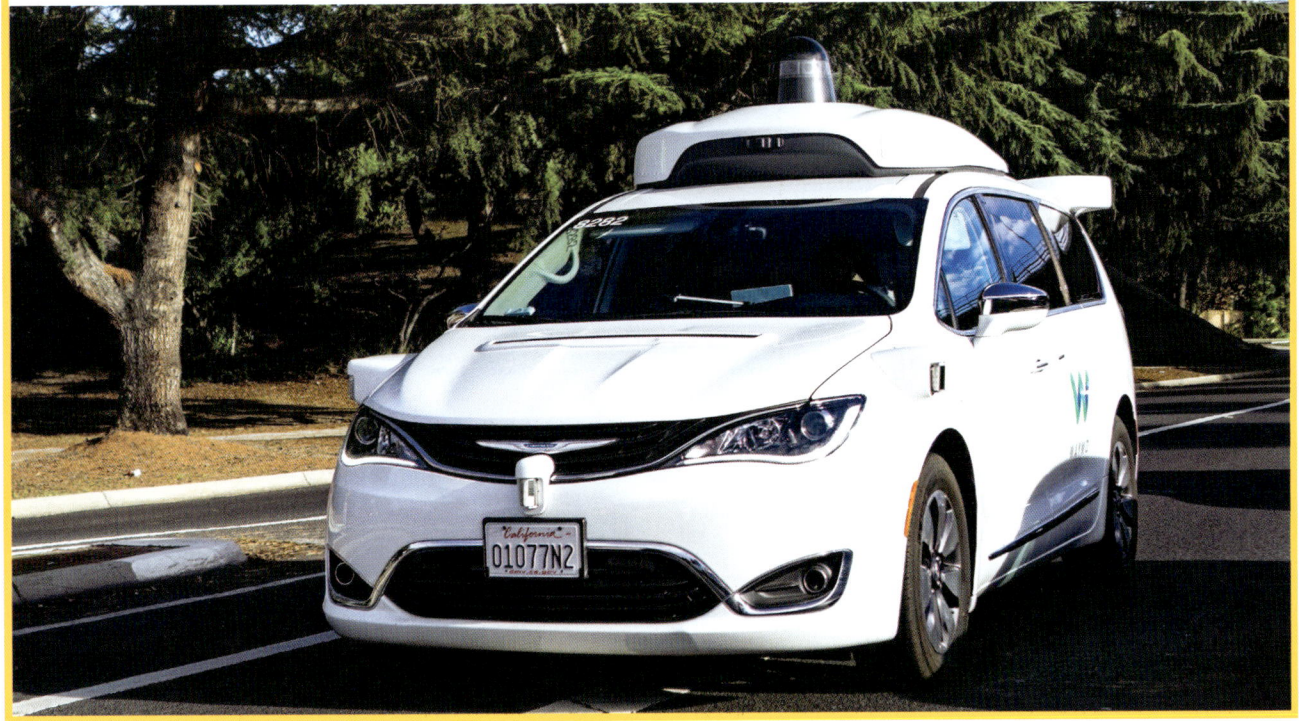

4 Computer systems

Unplugged activity 2

My robot helper

> **You will need:**
> pencils and paper, or a whiteboard pen and mini whiteboard

Design a robot to complete an everyday job around your home, or to help someone.

Marcus has an idea for his robot.

Draw your robot.

Write or say what your robot would do to help.

My robot would carry heavy shopping bags for people.

How are we doing?

Complete this sentence to explain why your device is a robot:

My device is a robot because …

Share your sentence with a partner.
Is their sentence similar to yours?

Look what I can do!

- ☐ I can name everyday devices that are controlled by computers.
- ☐ I can explain what a robot is.
- ☐ I can give examples of real robots.

4.3 Bots everywhere!

> **Project**
>
> **Make a poster to sell your robot!**
>
> > You will need:
> > a desktop computer, laptop or tablet with internet access, website link from your teacher or the Digital Learner's Book
>
> You have designed a robot.
>
> Now you are going to make a poster to help sell your robot.
>
> You are going to use a paint app to make your poster.
>
> On your poster:
> - have a drawing of your robot
> - tell people what the robot does.
>
> Here is the poster that Marcus made. 
>
> In groups:
> - talk about the posters you have made
> - choose a robot to tell your class about
> - explain to the class what your robot does to help.
>
> Have a class vote. Which robot would you buy?

This robot carries your heavy shopping for you!

4 Computer systems

Check your progress

1 Zara is trying to remember different types of computers.

 Help Zara by naming two other types of computer.

One type of computer is a desktop computer.

2 What do we call programs on tablets or phones?
 Choose the correct answer.

 A apps   B inputs   C control

3 Why do computers use different programs?
 Choose the correct answer.

 A So you can only do one thing with the computer.

 B So that you can do different things on the computer.

 C So that you can control where the mouse moves on the screen.

4 Arun is trying to remember how we get information into computers.

 Point to one thing we use to get information into a computer.

Continued

5 Name one way that a computer outputs information to us.

6 Some devices use computers to control what they do.

Which of these devices does not have a computer inside it? Choose the correct answer.

A car

B pedal scooter

C traffic lights

Glossary

algorithm	a set of instructions	11
	Zara followed the algorithm to build the model.	
app (short for application)	a computer program that does certain tasks	118
	The app on my brother's smartphone lets him play word games.	
bug	an error in a program or algorithm	52
	The bug in the Bee-Bot program made the Bee-Bot go the wrong way.	
code	instructions written in a special language that a computer program can understand	26
	Marcus checked that the code he had programmed was correct.	
collect	to gather	76
	We collect data by asking questions.	
command	an instruction that tells a computer what to do	25
	Sofia used the X command to clear her Bee-Bot's memory.	
connect	to join with something else	93
	Arun is going to connect his computer to a printer.	
control	getting something to do what you want	136
	Devices use special computers to control what they do.	
data	a piece of data is a fact — it can be a word, number or picture	66
	Zara puts data in the table.	

debugging	finding and fixing errors in a computer program or algorithm	52
	We are debugging our program because it isn't working properly.	
desktop computer	a computer that you cannot easily carry with you	94
	There is a desktop computer on the table.	
device	a piece of equipment that performs a task or a group of tasks	93
	A digital alarm clock is a very useful device.	
directions	instructions to make something move	20
	Arun gave his friend directions to his house.	
error	something that is not correct; a mistake	13
	I corrected the error in my work.	
form	a list of questions for people to answer	76
	I filled out the form online.	
games console	a computer that is mainly used for playing games	114
	Sofia likes playing on her games console.	
information	the collection of data with meaning	126
	The information on this web page is all about computers.	
input	to send something into a device	126
	Arun used the keyboard to input his password.	
instructions	a set of words or pictures that tell you what to do or how to make something work	9
	Sofia checked the instructions to find out how to play the game.	

internet	a network of many computers connected together across the world	103
	Arun uses the internet to speak to his grandparents because they live in a different country.	
keyboard	a set of keys that you press to type words and numbers into a computer	125
	Sofia used the keyboard to type her story.	
laptop	a computer that you can carry; it is flat when you close it	94
	Sofia's mum takes a laptop to work with her.	
list	a set of answers to choose from when answering a question	77
	I chose an answer from the list when I was using a form.	
mouse	a device that moves the arrow around a computer screen to click on things	125
	Marcus used the mouse to click on the video he wanted to play.	
network	two or more computers that are joined together	95
	My computer, tablet and smartphone are all part of the same network.	
offline	not connected to the internet	107
	Arun could not play his game because his laptop was offline.	
online	connected to the internet	107
	Marcus and Zara were both online so they did their homework together.	
output	when a device sends out information	132
	The speakers output the video's sound.	

personal data	information about yourself, like your name, age and where you live	67
	You should never share personal data with people you do not know.	
predict	to think about what will happen	45
	I predict that the Bee-Bot will turn right.	
printer	a device that can take images and text from the computer and put them on paper.	94
	The children used a printer to print out their stories.	
program (noun)	a list of instructions that makes a computer do a task	45
	You can use this program to make a drawing.	
program (verb)	putting a list of instructions into a computer to make it do a task	24
	Sofia wants to program the Bee-Bot to move forwards.	
robot	a device that does jobs without lots of help from humans	138
	The farm uses a robot to look for weeds.	
run	if you run the code, you tell the computer to carry out the instructions you have given it	42
	Zara programmed the Bee-Bot and then pressed GO to run her code.	
sequence	the order that things are in	12
	The beads were put into a sequence to make a pattern.	
smartphone	these are phones that can be carried around and used like a computer.	94
	Zara's sister has a smartphone so she can message her friends.	

sort	look for something that is the same	71
	Marcus is going to sort the blocks into different colours.	
speaker	a device that outputs sound	132
	Arun listened to music using the computer's speakers.	
table	where data is put to make it easier to use	66
	Putting the data in the table made it easier to answer the question.	
tablet	a small, very portable computer	94
	Arun watches videos on his tablet.	
touchscreen	a computer screen which also acts as an input	127
	Sofia used the touchscreen to zoom in on the photo.	
wi-fi	the common wireless connection in our homes and school	98
	Sofia and Arun use wi-fi to share information between their computers.	
wireless	when a computer or device does not need a wire to connect to a network	98
	This tablet makes a wireless connection to the network.	

Acknowledgements

The authors and publishers acknowledge the following sources of copyright material and are grateful for the permissions granted. While every effort has been made, it has not always been possible to identify the sources of all the material used, or to trace all copyright holders. If any omissions are brought to our notice, we will be happy to include the appropriate acknowledgements on reprinting.

Thanks to the following for permission to reproduce images:

Unit 1: John M Lund Photography Inc/GI; Westend61/GI; Phynart Studio/GI; FatCamera/GI; l000pixels/GI; OlgaKhorkova/Shutterstock; JasonDoiy/GI; Klaus Vedfelt/GI; Clover No.7 Photography/GI; Klaus Vedfelt/GI; BraunS/GI; Mode Images/Alamy Stock Photo; Jonathan Kirn/GI; Don Farrall/GI; Radu Dumitrescu/GI; Manoj Mugri/GI; SDI Productions/GI; Sandra standbridge/GI;Peter Dazeley/GI; Andersen Ross Photography Inc/GI; Wmarkusen/GI; **Unit 2:** Marc Romanelli/GI; Giuseppe Lombardo/EyeEm/GI; Mensent Photography/GI; Spanteldotru/GI; Stockcam/GI; David Leahy/GI; Nenov/GI; Matthew Horwood/GI; Nick Dolding/GI; Petr Pikora/GI; Creativeye99/GI; Eric Schaeffer/GI; FatCamera/GI; NanoStockk/GI; Kontrec/GI; Gerdtromm/GI; OrangeDukeProductions/GI; Bubaone/GI; Appleuzr/GI; Andersen Ross Photography Inc/GI; aluxum/GI; Diane555/GI (x6); Sean Gladwell/GI; Klaus Vedfelt/GI; Thomas Barwick/GI; Marc Romanelli/GI; Diane555/GI (x2); Matthias Kulka/GI; Id-work/GI; RobinOlimb/GI; Roi and Roi/GI; **Unit 3:** Klaus Vedfelt/GI; Skynesher/GI; Leonello calvetti /GI; Richard Newstead/GI; GeniusKp/GI; Rose_Carson/GI; Jeffrey Coolidge/GI; DmitriyKazitsyn/GI; Archive Photos/GI; Popovaphoto/GI; Carol Yepes/GI; Thomas Barwick/GI; Tetra Images/GI; Alexandra Draghici/GI; adventtr/GI; Cginspiration/GI; Suriyo Hmun Kaew/GI; Phynart Studio/GI; Mint Images/GI; Morsa Images/GI; Blend Images - JGI/Jamie Grill/GI; Yagi Studio/GI; Oscar Wong/GI; daboost/GI; Pongnathee Kluaythong/GI; Arnon Mungyodklang/GI; Jeffrey Coolidge/GI; Javier Zayas Photography/GI; Sweetym/GI; Jill Ferry Photography/GI; Tom Werner/GI; **Unit 4:** Carol Yepes/GI; Ariel Skelley/GI; Marko Geber/GI; Hello Africa/GI; Mayur Kakade/GI; daboost/GI; Jeffrey Coolidge/GI; Daboost/GI; Scanrail/GI; Tobias Titz/GI; Studiogstock/GI; Tim Platt/GI; Fancy Yan/GI; Opka/GI; Stockcam/GI; Issarawat Tattong/GI; Sally Anscombe/GI; Westend61/GI; Peter Cade/GI; Ilkercelik/GI; Mehdi fedouach/GI; Martial Colomb/GI; SpiffyJ/GI; Jamie Grill/GI; Colorblind Images LLC/GI; John Lamb/GI; LordRunar/GI; Peter Dazeley/GI; Small Robot Company; Andrey Bryzgalov/GI; EthamPhoto/GI; Sundry Photography/GI; Thana Prasongsin/GI; Barry Wong/GI; Ariel Skelley/GI; Stockcam/GI; Amnachphoto/GI; Henrik5000/GI; ValuaVitaly/GI; rzelich/GI

Key: GI = Getty Images

Cover image by Pablo Gallego (Beehive Illustration)

Bee-Bot is a registered trade mark of RM Resources. Illustrations depicting Bee-Bots are created with permission of RM Resources.